8 STEPS
to Create the
Life You
Want

8 STEPS
to Create the
Life You Want

The Anatomy of a Successful Life

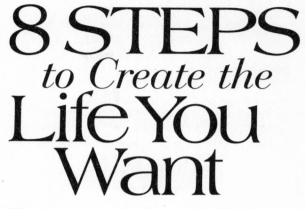

DR. CREFLO A. DOLLAR

NEW YORK   BOSTON   NASHVILLE

Unless otherwise indicated, Scriptures are taken from the King James Version (KJV).

Scriptures noted AMP are taken from The Amplified® Bible. Copyright © 1954, 1962, 1965, 1987 by The Lockman Foundation. Used by permission.

Scriptures noted NIV are taken from the HOLY BIBLE: NEW INTERNATIONAL VERSION®. Copyright © 1973, 1978, 1984 by International Bible Society. Used by permission of Zondervan Publishing House. All rights reserved.

Scriptures noted NLT are from the *Holy Bible*, New Living Translation, copyright © 1996. Used by permission of Tyndale House Publishers, Inc., Wheaton, Illinois 60189. All rights reserved.

Scriptures noted The Message are taken from The Message. Copyright © 1993, 1994, 1995, 1996, 2000, 2001, 2002. Used by permission of NavPress Publishing Group.

FaithWords
Hachette Book Group
237 Park Avenue
New York, NY 10017

Visit our Web site at www.faithwords.com.

Printed in the United States of America

Originally published in hardcover by Hachette Book Group.

First Trade Edition: January 2009

10 9 8 7 6 5 4 3

FaithWords is a division of Hachette Book Group, Inc.
The FaithWords name and logo are trademarks of Hachette Book Group, Inc.

The Library of Congress has cataloged the hardcover edition as follows:

Dollar, Creflo A.
8 steps to create the life you want : the anatomy of a
successful life / Creflo A. Dollar.—1st ed.
p. cm.
Includes bibliographical references.
ISBN-13: 978-0-446-58070-0
ISBN-10: 0-446-58070-8
1. Success—Religious aspects—Christianity.   I. Title.   II. Title: Eight
steps to create the life you want.
BV4598.3.D64 2008
248.4—dc22
2007011215

ISBN 978-0-446-69964-8 (pbk.)

With much prayer and seeking God as to the message and direction He wanted to take this project, I realized just how much of a support my wife, Taffi, has been in my life. It was she who walked these steps out with me as we grew in Christ.

Taffi, it is no light thing for me to realize the good thing that I have found in you, and the favor I have obtained from the Lord (Proverbs 18:22). Because of your faith in and obedience to our heavenly Father, and because of your belief in me, I was able to achieve this. As I worked through this book, you demonstrated your confidence in me by submitting to me as I submit to Christ. For that I thank you.

You not only understand the anatomy of life, but you have helped me understand and move into each new level that God has taken us. You are the love of my life. It is with all these things in mind that I dedicate this entire work to you! I love you.

In whom also we have obtained an inheritance, being predestinated according to the purpose of him who worketh all things after the counsel of his own will: That we should be to the praise of his glory, who first trusted in Christ.

Ephesians 1:11–12

Contents

Acknowledgments

I would like to acknowledge my in-house editorial staff: To the Senior Editor of Books, Carmen Glover: the countless hours you spent working on and supervising this project will always be appreciated. Thank you for leading a dynamic team by example. You are an asset to the ministry, and your team is a reflection of all that you are.

To the editors: Yolanda Harris, Suzanne Mohr, Hope Christmas, Cheesette Stovall, Tawanda Mills, and Annette Davis: I appreciate your making this project a success by allowing the Holy Spirit to creatively funnel His anointing *through you*, into this project, every step of the way.

To the proofreaders: Cheesette Stovall, Hope Christmas, Annette Davis, Eric Strickland, and Tawanda Mills: Thank you for your skilled and sharp eyes.

To the entire publications team: I thank each of you for humbly submitting to God, working as unto Him to make this project a success. Each of you has meaningfully impacted this project. I appreciate your contributions in completing this project. Your support of the vision God has given me for this ministry proves your faithfulness to the Kingdom of God.

A great project is reflective of the efforts of great people, but a work of art is a great reflection of their hearts.

Words alone cannot express how grateful I am for you and your willing hearts!

Introduction

We all want to enjoy a great life, and after years of studying God's Word, I have uncovered a proven process that will lead to a life of success and total fulfillment. I believe that, when applied, the steps outlined in this book will revolutionize your life and change even the most difficult situations.

As we strive to better ourselves and achieve our goals, it can be frustrating at times to watch other people enjoying life as we and others around us struggle. Perhaps you're trying to launch a business, purchase a home, or recover from a financial setback, but it seems that every time you take one step forward, you fall two steps backward. Let me encourage you today: those days are over! Draw a line in the sand; you're about to cross over into new territory! I'm about to introduce to you a brand new approach to life that will ultimately lead you to your divine destination.

No matter how things appear today, I want you to remember this: God wants *you* to live the good life! In fact, Jesus reveals this truth in Ephesians 2:10. It confirms that before you were born, God determined your purpose and created a path that would lead you to "the good life which He prearranged and made ready for you to live" (AMP).

This Scripture also affirms that through Christ, we are born anew, that we may do the "good works" the Father planned for us long before we were ever born. The good works He refers to in Ephesians specifically relate to your life's purpose. They are those things you were called to do and enjoy even if no one paid you to do them. And there are specific paths that you must take to arrive at the place God has already prepared.

Plain and simple; God has a prescribed plan for your life, an appointed purpose and destiny that He established from the beginning.

God has provided a wealth of wisdom, knowledge, and direction in His Word to assist us in arriving at our destination. When we don't subscribe to God's plan, we postpone our progress and set ourselves up for disappointment and discouragement. As a result, we go through life constantly searching for answers to questions like, "What am I here for?" and "Which path should I take?" when God has already provided the answers.

Part of the process of reaching your destination and being successful is recognizing that *you* have a part to play. So many people "wait on God" to take them to their place of fulfillment in life, and then blame Him when they fail. Others consider the Bible to be some sort of magic book of promises. They want only to name it and claim it, believe it and receive it, then go, "Poof . . . there it is!" But there's so much more! People who think this way somehow convince themselves that God will magically fix their situation. Here's a news flash: God isn't into magic tricks! He has a master plan and *your* job is to operate within that plan.

There are also people on the opposite extreme. They don't see the need to get God involved in their decisions at all. Rather than seeking Him for guidance, they rely on their experience, education, and networking skills to lead them to the path of success.

I often hear people say, "What's meant to be, will be," but that just doesn't line up with Scripture. Your *decisions* are what create your reality; nothing just *happens.* The truth is, until you identify God's plan for your life and understand the *process* that leads to your destination, you will either delay or forfeit the good life He has planned for you.

The goal of this book is to help you gain a greater awareness of that process and the factors that lead to your desired end. I will show you, step by step, how to achieve success, enrich your life, and discover your life's purpose. As a result, you will improve your well-being and experience fulfillment in your career, relationships, and future endeavors.

As you read each chapter and complete the practical application exercises, I encourage you to open your heart and mind to the new direction in which God may be leading you. No matter where you are today, regardless of the decisions you made yesterday, there is hope. Today is a new day filled with opportunity. Your whole way of thinking is about to change. Get ready for it. Life can be as good as you make it, so make it good!

If you're ready to experience God's best, and walk out His plan for your life, get your pen and paper and let's take this journey together. The good life is available to you *now*! Step into it.

Step 1

Revolutionize
Your Words

The Power of Decision

When I was a child and my friends and I wanted to choose who would play on our team during a game, or who would go first in a certain activity, we would point to each person as we chanted the following rhyme:

> Eenie, meenie, miney, mo; catch a monkey by his toe.
> If he hollers, let him go. Eenie, meenie, miney, mo.

When the rhyme ended, whoever stood in the direction of the pointed finger was designated as the chosen one. Sometimes the choice proved favorable, and sometimes it didn't. Though this haphazard method was fine for children's games, it doesn't work well for real-life decisions. Yet, amazingly, some adults still subscribe to this childlike method when making decisions.

Former First Lady Eleanor Roosevelt once said:

> One's philosophy is not best expressed in words; it is expressed in the choices one makes. In the long run, we shape our lives and we shape ourselves. The process never ends until we die. And the choices we make are ultimately our own responsibility.

Life is a serious matter, and decisions must not be made carelessly. The choices we make today determine not only where we will end up tomorrow, but also where we'll be years down the road. Every decision impacts our success, happiness, health, and overall well-being. Our choices also impact the lives of others, including our families, coworkers, and communities. We must accept the responsibility for our choices and refuse to blame others for the unfortunate things we experience. We must examine our present circumstances and ask ourselves, "What role have I played in making my life what it is today?" If we're honest, we will realize that our happiness and success, or lack thereof, are directly related to specific decisions we've made over the course of time.

LIFE IS A SERIES OF DECISIONS

Our decisions cause us to take certain actions, which in turn lead to certain habits that shape our character and impact our destination. A Believer's decisions must be wise and biblically based, rather than based on emotions. This is a fundamental key to walking in the plan God has established for our lives.

You may know people who say they are going to start a new project, lose weight, or break some habit, yet never follow through. People talk a great deal about what they *want* to do, but very few employ the tenacity and diligence required to carry it out. They need to stop talking about it and just do it!

Everything starts with a decision. Look at the number of couples who get married, vowing to stick together through sickness and health, for richer or poorer, until death do they part, only to end up in divorce court, pointing fingers at one another over why things went wrong. What prevents them from keeping their vows? I am convinced it is because most divorced couples operated in human, emotional love, rather than unconditional love during their marriage. God teaches us to avoid being judgmental, finding fault, and refusing to forgive. When faced with conflict, a married person's ideal response should be, "I'm with you, and I'm going to keep on loving you no matter what!"

The God kind of love is called *agape* love. It's based on a decision, not a feeling. Allowing our feelings to govern our decisions is like being tossed by every wind. We shouldn't make decisions that way. Instead, our decisions and emotions should be firmly based on and supported by the Word of God. This is the only way to guarantee success in marriage, in life, and in every aspect of our being.

There is a difference between making a decision and making a *quality* decision. A quality decision is a choice that matches God's desires for your life. It moves you to take a specific corresponding action. For example, if a sexually promiscuous person learns that premarital sex is not the will of God, and makes a quality decision to align his life with God's plan, he will take the necessary steps to enforce that decision. This involves establishing new boundaries and adopting a disciplined mindset. This decision will require taking a stand even in the face of criticism from others. It may seem difficult at first, but pleasing God is worth it.

There is a difference between making a decision and making a quality *decision.*

Correcting any former practice, whether it's overeating, lying, cheating, or becoming angry, requires separation from old habits and routines that could undermine your decision. I know people who say they've kicked the smoking habit, but they still go on break with people who smoke. Eventually, the person who made the quality decision not to smoke will end up smoking again. It's inevitable. I once had a problem with eating too many donuts. In order to overcome in that area, I stopped driving by the donut shop every day, especially when the "Hot" sign flashed in the window, indicating fresh donuts were available! I changed my routine in order to protect my decision.

Not only do you need to change your old patterns, you need to create new habits. You can't keep doing things the old way and expect to get different results. Establish new personal boundaries. Get God involved. Ask the Holy Spirit to help you when temptations come. No matter how big or small the problem, you *can* overcome it with God's help. God is committed to helping you claim His promises.

The Gospels are full of stories about people who made quality decisions to believe Jesus for what they needed. Mark 5:25–34 documents the account of a woman who had an illness that caused her to have a continuous hemorrhage for twelve years. She sought help from many physicians, to no avail. When she heard that Jesus would be passing through her town, she realized He was the answer to her dilemma. When she stepped out in faith and touched His garment, she was completely healed!

Reaching out to touch Jesus was not a socially acceptable decision in that culture at that time. I'm sure she realized she was taking quite a chance. In fact, by touching Jesus, she put her life on the line. In that day, women who were on their menstrual cycles weren't allowed in public. She could have been legally stoned! However, her decision to believe in Jesus' healing power, along with her corresponding action to tap into His power, led to a miracle. Likewise, when you tap into Jesus' miracle-working power, you, too, can expect things to change.

Making a quality decision is seldom easy. It may require you to step out of your comfort zone, go against the expectations of well-meaning family members and friends, and stand alone. The good news is, when your decisions line up with the Word of God, Heaven supports you. Every quality decision you make opens the door for Jesus, the Holy Spirit, and the angels to get involved in your circumstances. Just as the woman with the issue of blood initiated her own miracle, you must also initiate restoration and wholeness in your own life by making quality decisions supported by corresponding actions.

When your decisions line up with the Word of God, Heaven supports you.

Stay on guard! Once you decide to base all your choices on the truth of God's Word, Satan will show up to try to change your mind. Don't allow him to distract you. Maintain your stance. Have faith that every decision you make is divinely directed by the Word of God.

LOCATE THE WILL OF GOD

Learning how to make good choices starts with learning God's will. His will is His Word. Meditate on it; then read it again. Even before you know God's specific purpose for your life, making the choice to live by

His Word will position you in His will. The great thing about discovering God's will and making godly decisions is that it ultimately leads you to the right destination. When you find out what the Word says, you will know exactly what you need to do to obtain total-life prosperity.

> *When you find out what the Word says, you will know exactly what you need to do to obtain total-life prosperity.*

Whether it is a career choice, a relationship choice, or a decision concerning your health, there is a Bible-based answer for every situation you face in life. How can you receive healing if you don't know what God says in His Word about it? How can you be wealthy if you don't know what the Word says about wealth and prosperity? How can you have a successful marriage if you don't know what the Word says about marriage and the role each spouse plays? When you take the time to read and study the Bible, you not only learn who God is and what His will is for your life, you also learn who you are! As His child, you are entitled to every benefit and privilege that your relationship with Him allows. The blessings available are endless! In Him you are able to accomplish all things simply because He says so. In fact, this is confirmed several times in Scripture:

"I can do all things through Christ which strengtheneth me" (Philippians 4:13).

"With God all things are possible" (Matthew 19:26).

"If thou canst believe, all things are possible" (Mark 9:23).

God wants you to experience His goodness every day. That is why it is important that you live a life that is pleasing to Him and make choices He can support you in. Even in the midst of difficulties or when you're feeling overwhelmed by life's many demands, resist the temptation to do things your way.

> *God wants you to experience His goodness every day.*

Luke 10:38–42 tells the story of two sisters, Mary and Martha. As Jesus and His disciples were visiting them one day, Jesus began to teach.

Mary sat at Jesus' feet, listening to what He had to say. Martha, on the other hand, was distracted by the demands of cooking and serving the group. Martha became annoyed because Mary wouldn't help her in the kitchen. In fact, she was so upset that she complained to Jesus and asked Him to tell Mary to help her. Jesus said, "Martha, Martha, thou art careful and troubled about many things: But one thing is needful: and Mary hath chosen that good part, which shall not be taken away from her" (Luke 10:41, 42). In other words, Martha's decision to become bogged down with cooking and serving wasn't a quality decision. However, Mary did the needful thing by sitting at Jesus' feet to receive His wisdom and instruction.

Sitting at the Lord's feet and learning from Him are the most important things you can ever do. Your daily conversations with God will yield the answers you seek. He wants to talk with you. Spend time in His presence, fellowshiping with Him in prayer and receiving His direction for each day. Be sure you don't spend all your prayer time listing requests. Discipline yourself to be quiet and receive His response as well.

Time with God shouldn't be something you just fit into your schedule. Neither should it be something you do only when you have a need. It should be a daily priority. Your thinking should be: "God first . . . then everything else." I assure you, your life will be a lot more rewarding when you give Him first place.

Life will be a lot more rewarding when you give God first place.

God wants to get involved in every area of your life, but He can't if you make choices without Him. If you choose to do things your way or continue to pursue something you shouldn't, you won't position yourself to receive the promise. Decisions made outside of God's will prevent Him from getting involved.

Sometimes in situations that seem small and harmless, disobedience and deceit show up in order to rob us of our blessings. The "little foxes" referred to in Song of Solomon 2:15, are the ones you have to look out for. Constantly reminding your children of their past mistakes, gossiping with coworkers, and making fun of people are all little foxes that have the power to negatively impact your life. Always be on the lookout for the little foxes. You'll be surprised by what you find, and by the blessings that flow when you trap those foxes with God's Word.

Jonah had the opportunity to make a quality decision, but failed to obey God in something as small as taking a trip to another city. God told Jonah to go to Nineveh, a wicked city where sin prevailed, and preach to the people. Jonah, well aware of the magnitude of wickedness that existed in Nineveh, decided to disobey God and fled by ship to a different city. His decision led him away from the will of God.

While Jonah traveled to Nineveh, "the LORD sent out a great wind into the sea, and there was a mighty tempest in the sea, so that the ship was like to be broken" (Jonah 1:4). Everyone on board was in danger of losing his life! When the other travelers discovered that Jonah was the cause of God's wrath, he was tossed overboard and swallowed by a great fish.

Jonah's emotions caused him to make a decision that took him out of the will of God. In addition, Jonah's decision endangered the lives of those around him. Eventually, God redeemed Jonah and forgave Him for his disobedience. Jonah ultimately fulfilled the will of God for His life, but it cost him something. Had he done what God said the first time, he would have avoided misfortune and positioned himself for God's perfect will rather than His permissive will. You see, we enjoy the benefits of God's perfect will when we immediately cooperate with His plans. Permissive will is when we do things our way, eventually figure out that it's the wrong way, repent, and get back on track.

Many people are like Jonah. I know; I've been there. God would tell me to do one thing, and I would do another. I made decisions out of God's will on many occasions as a pastor, father, husband, and businessman. Eventually I realized that I wasn't as smart as God and made a quality decision to avoid making choices that were outside of His will for my life. That decision has put me on the path to my destiny. The moment I made the decision to repent and start doing things God's way, He led me out of my error and into His will.

THE GREAT LIFE

There is a life far greater than you could ever imagine. To live it, you must be willing to pursue the will of God in every decision. Here are some practical ways to make the right decisions and fulfill God's will for your life:

1. Surrender all of your plans to the Lord.

Apply the Scriptures to your life and situations. When you do, the Holy Spirit will speak to you. I've heard Him speak to me when I didn't want to be spoken to, especially when I wanted to yield to emotions that were leading me in the wrong direction. I've learned, however, that His words will always save me from destruction.

2. Surround yourself with godly men and women, and imitate their faith and good character.

If you want to be an eagle, you can't stay in the chicken coop. Find someone who's doing what you want to do, living the life you want to live, and getting results. Try to make contact with that person and establish a relationship. If you're unable to make contact, research his history. See what roles faith and character play in his life and business. Learn what he did to get to where he is and imitate those things. Don't lose yourself in the process. Apply what you learn, and become a better you. Soon you'll be doing what you were called to do.

3. Set aside time daily to pray and study God's Word.

If you'll begin your day by setting aside fifteen minutes to pray, and gradually increase it as the weeks progress, you'll receive all the wisdom and direction you need.

4. Ask the Lord to reveal His will in every situation you encounter.

James 1:5 says, "If any of you lacks wisdom, he should ask God, who gives generously to all without finding fault, and it will be given to him" (NIV). Realize that you need God's wisdom and direction both to find and to live in His will. God has a solution for even the smallest problems you face. He wants to be intimately involved in your life. Let Him.

5. Use Scriptures as the foundation for how you live.

Find Scriptures to support whatever you need God to do in your life. Confess those Scriptures daily until your heart and mind come into complete agreement with them. When you pray, recite the Scriptures to God because God's Word never returns void. It accomplishes everything! You are guaranteed results when you pray His Word. "So shall my word be that goeth forth out of my mouth: it shall not return unto me void, but it shall accomplish that which I please, and it shall prosper in the thing whereto I sent it" (Isaiah 55:11).

6. Don't be swayed by your emotions or the pressures of life.

Emotions aren't bad. In fact, every emotion has its place. You must, however, rule over them and not allow them to rule over you. When life gets you in a pinch, don't react. Instead, respond. Don't let pressure move you. Stay focused, and never make decisions when you are emotional. Consult God, and after receiving His direction, move forward.

7. Be willing to learn from your mistakes.

Some of the best lessons I've learned have come as a result of falling flat on my face. We shouldn't condemn ourselves for our mistakes because God never does. In fact, Scripture says that there is no condemnation for those who are in Christ (Romans 8:1). When you make a wrong turn in life, go back and analyze the decisions you made that led you in that direction. Reevaluate the thinking you had during that time. Once you know what went wrong, it will be much easier to make it right the next time. Be humble and put away your pride. Don't allow past mistakes, or the people who remind you of them, to get you down or off track. Learn the lesson and keep moving forward.

YOU'VE GOT THE POWER

J. Martin Kohe wrote in his book, *Your Greatest Power*, "The greatest power that a person possesses is the power to choose." If you want to avoid the pitfalls of life, you must learn how to make the right decisions, at the right time. You can do this by consistently seeking God's Word and His guidance before you make decisions. Before making a move, find out what God has to say about your situation. You'll find peace like you've never known.

Here are eight key questions to ask yourself when making decisions:

1. What are the possible consequences of my decision?
2. How will my decision affect the lives of others?
3. Will my decision influence me to be disobedient to God?
4. Have I sought godly counsel regarding this situation?
5. Will my decision promote the love of God?
6. Will God bless and approve of my decision?
7. Will I be able to thank God for the outcome of my decision?
8. Will my decision bring glory and honor to God?

God has given you the power to choose, but I encourage you to use that power wisely. The next time you are faced with a decision, make a checklist using the above questions, read God's Word, and ask the Holy Spirit to speak to you about your situation. In doing so, you will form a habit of making decisions that please God and place you on the path to your destiny.

Review Nuggets

Life is a series of decisions. Your present circumstances can be traced back to the decisions you've made. If you want to live a happy, healthy, and fulfilling life, locate the will of God before making a decision.

Once you've made a decision, set boundaries that will ensure that you are able to carry out the plan you have established. Every quality decision you make based on the Word will be supported by God and His angels. He will ensure your success.

Foundation Scripture

If any of you lacks wisdom, he should ask God, who gives generously to all without finding fault, and it will be given to him.

James 1:5 (NIV)

Practical Application

Get out your journal and divide one of the pages into two columns. Identify areas in your life where you have made bad choices and write them down in the left column. Then go to the Word and find Scriptures that you can use to make better decisions. Write them in the second column. Now look up Scriptures that pertain to seeking God and obtaining wisdom. Apply these Scriptures to situations you may be facing now, and ask God to lead you in your decision-making process. Write down what He tells you to do for each situation. Base your choices on what the Word says, and write down what you will do to maintain and protect your decision. Refer to your list daily.

The Best Decision
You'll Ever Make

In life, there are decisions that must be made every day, and although you may not want to make them, you must. Accepting Jesus as your Lord and Savior is one decision that not only affects your life now, it impacts your eternal destination. It is the best, and most important decision you will ever make. Choosing to accept Jesus into your heart and making the Bible your final authority are the first major steps on the way to your destination. Without salvation, you may find yourself wandering through life, never quite knowing your purpose. Or you may find yourself achieving success the world's way, but paying a price for it later.

Perhaps you've heard such phrases as, "I got saved" or "I was born again." You may have grown up hearing those types of phrases without *really* understanding what they meant, or knowing that they referred to salvation. *Salvation* comes from the Greek word *soteria*, which means, "wholeness, deliverance, victory, prosperity, health and welfare" (blueletterbible.org). Salvation encompasses every area of your life, from your spiritual condition to relationships and finances. It is a free gift that you receive by faith, and it's much more than a "fire insurance policy" or deliverance from eternal separation from God. While your eternal destination is of huge importance, God is equally concerned about how you live while here on Earth. Accepting Jesus positions you to receive the benefits of Heaven after you die. It also gives you access to abundant life on Earth.

Today's society believes, "If it feels good, do it." That mindset would have you believe it doesn't matter whether you make the decision to accept Jesus into your life, or that being a Christian is a waste of time. That simply is not true.

In John 3:3, Jesus says that being born again is the *only* way a man can enter the Kingdom of God. This contradicts the *all-inclusive* message that says, "All roads lead to God." The choice is yours. You have to choose what you will believe.

Being born again obviously doesn't mean a physical rebirth. It means that when you accept Jesus into your heart by faith, your spiritual condition changes—your spirit man is recreated. You become a new creation that has never existed. When you accept Christ, you no longer have to remain enslaved to sin. He is your way out!

When you make this life-changing decision, you are making a quality decision to turn away from sin and develop a personal relationship with God through His Son, Jesus. Many people have become acquainted with traditional religion—they believe in God and may even go to church out of family tradition or obligation. They may know all the "churchy" things to say or do that they think will make them right with God. However, there is a difference between religion and *relationship*. God wants every person to have intimate fellowship with Him. This type of fellowship is possible only by accepting His Son, Jesus, as the overseer of your life.

Think about the relationships you have with loved ones. You would probably agree it took time to cultivate trust and love with them. By spending time with one another and going through different experiences together, you were able to create a relationship that has meaning, purpose, and fulfillment. The same is true with God. Jesus is God's way of reaching out to you. When you receive Jesus into your life, you have an avenue to connect with the heavenly Father. You will experience the best relationship you've ever known by spending time with God through prayer, reading and meditating on His Word, and allowing Him to show Himself strong on your behalf.

There is a spiritual void that exists in the lives of people who are not born again. As a result, many seek satisfaction and fulfillment through people, success, and material acquisitions. However, those things will never satisfy the deep longing that can be fulfilled only by a spiritual connection to God. You may spend your life trying to attain or achieve something you think will make you happy, but God is the only one who can fill the empty space inside you.

God is the only one who can fill the empty space inside you.

SALVATION: A KEY TO UNLOCKING YOUR DESTINY

Becoming a Christian is the first key to opening the door to your God-ordained destiny. There are those who say, "It doesn't take all that to be successful." However, true success is found in God and His way of doing things. You will experience lasting fulfillment when everything you do is founded on God's Word. With Jesus all things are possible.

People who are unsaved have no reference point from which to make sound decisions. Their decisions are based on emotions, reason, or intellect. With each decision, they step out on a limb and hope things will work out. If things go well, they ascribe it to being "lucky." If things don't go well, they blame bad luck or believe "it just wasn't meant to be."

You don't have to base your life on a luck system when you're a part of God's system. In God's Kingdom, faith is the currency, and positive results are guaranteed every time you obey Him and abide by the principles in His Word.

Positive results are guaranteed every time you obey God and abide by the principles in His Word.

Believers have a foolproof way to live successfully every day of their lives. Once you accept Jesus into your life, His Holy Spirit comes and dwells inside you. He knows the steps you must take to reach your destiny, and if you listen to Him, you can't go wrong. He is there to teach, instruct, help, and direct you (John 14:26). As you learn to recognize, listen to, and obey His voice, you are able to walk in God's path for your life with guaranteed success.

Proverbs 20:27 says, "The spirit of man is the candle of the LORD." That means that as the Holy Spirit dwells in your spirit, He will lead you in the right direction. When the Holy Spirit directs your steps, you never have to grope around in darkness, trying to find your way. His guidance will be like the light of a candle that shows you which way to go and which decisions to make in every area of your life. This is vital when it comes to making decisions that will lead you into His perfect will.

Your relationship with God must be cultivated daily so you can learn to hear His voice, even regarding the minute details of your life. This is the benefit of being saved—you get the "inside scoop" on how to proceed in life without having to constantly learn from making the wrong decisions. Think about how great it is to have someone who knows all things teaching you what to do every step of the way! As you develop an intimate relationship with Him, you will experience a level of freedom and fulfillment you've never experienced before.

Another reason it is vital to be born again is because it moves you out of the dominion and authority of Satan's kingdom—the world's system. The world's system refers to the system of operation of those who do not know God. They aren't led by the Spirit of God. He isn't ordering their steps. This path eventually leads to sorrow and defeat.

THE HIGHER WAY OF LIFE

The world's system of operation is governed by fear, sin, and selfishness. This way of operating is under the dominion of the kingdom of darkness. Decisions and actions aren't aligned with the Bible. Therefore, those who operate under this system experience the negative results of their choices. But they have a choice in the matter! When you are born again, God snatches you out of Satan's clutches and moves you into His Kingdom (Colossians 1:13, 14). This is a higher way of life.

It's full of the blessings of God, including divine health, deliverance from danger through angelic protection, as well as spiritual and material riches.

There are people who say, "Where in the Bible does it say that it's God's will for us to prosper?" It's unfortunate that so many Christians have problems with prosperity because they can't see it clearly in the Word of God. The truth is, God has placed this promise throughout the Bible, and salvation is the first step. Third John 1:2 reads, "Beloved, I wish above all things that thou mayest prosper and be in health, even as thy soul prospereth." Prosperity is success and wholeness in every area of your life, including your relationships, health, work, and—yes—finances, although it isn't just about money.

The main reason for prosperity is so you can be a blessing to others (Genesis 12:2, 3). You cannot possibly be a blessing to anyone else if you are broke, busted, and disgusted! Psalm 35:27 says God takes pleasure in your prosperity. It's an expression of His love. Like you, He wants the best for His children.

The main reason for prosperity is so you can be a blessing to others.

Angelic assistance is another benefit of salvation. Angels are part of God's plan to bring you to your destination in life. Hebrews 1:13, 14 says, "But to which of the angels said he at any time, Sit on my right hand, until I make thine enemies thy footstool? Are they not all ministering spirits, sent forth to minister for them who shall be heirs of salvation?" Angels are servants, sent by God, on your behalf. Not only do they protect you, they help to usher you into your destiny.

When the Bible talks about *heirs*, it's talking about you! You are an heir of salvation. You are an heir to an inheritance. If you had a rich uncle who named you as the heir to his estate, everything he owned would be passed on to you. Likewise, when you accept Jesus as your personal Savior, you become an heir to every promise that God made to Abraham (Genesis 17:7).

WHOLENESS ON EVERY LEVEL

In Hebrew, the original language of the Old Testament, the word for salvation is *Yshuwah*. *Yshuwah* means deliverance, victory, prosperity, health, and welfare (*Strong's Concordance* definition 03444). So when God talks about salvation, He is addressing wholeness in your spirit, soul, and body. When you accept salvation, there is nothing missing or lacking in your life (1 Thessalonians 5:23). This is why accepting Jesus is so important. You can't be successful in reaching your destiny or a life of total fulfillment without Him.

In Luke 17:12–19, we read about ten lepers who were healed by Jesus. Although ten were healed, only one came back to say thank you. Jesus said something very interesting to the one who came back: "Thy faith hath made thee whole." Jesus healed the leprosy that afflicted all ten of the men, but He gave *wholeness* to the one who came back to praise God by faith. Healing was freely given to all ten, but faith restored what was lacking in the spirit, soul, and body of the one who recognized the source of his salvation.

Another illustration of this is the story I mentioned earlier of the woman with the issue of blood. Her faith that she could be healed by just touching the hem of Jesus' garment made her whole. When she touched Jesus, she was not only healed of her sickness, but Jesus said, "[Your] faith [has] made [you] whole." He healed everything in her life. Jesus restored her finances, lost relationships and everything that concerned her (Luke 8:43–48).

It's not enough to just be healed physically. God wants to restore everything that is lacking in your life. That's what salvation is all about. You have to *know* that you are His heir and participate in your God-given inheritance by increasing your faith and acting on His Word.

God wants to restore everything that is lacking in your life.

SPEAK TO YOUR CHALLENGES

As a Believer, you will encounter challenges as you walk out God's plan for your life. Satan will see to it. However, Satan won't succeed when you are confident in the salvation that God has afforded you through Jesus. When you take hold of the power God has given you, the devil doesn't stand a chance against you.

If you want to experience the victory that comes through salvation, start speaking God's Word all the time. Your victory is in what you speak, and when you speak God's Word, you tap into the salvation that is rightfully yours. If you want to get out of debt or have dreams of owning a business, find Scriptures on those things and say them until your heart becomes established in them. When you do this, you release a spiritual force that rearranges things in your life and causes the devil to back off when he tries to hinder that process.

Your healing, deliverance, and desires are wrapped up in your salvation. Salvation is much more than just forgiveness of sin and the born-again experience. God doesn't just deliver you from sin. He delivers you from sickness, addiction, poverty, and everything else the enemy tries to use to attack you.

Take a moment to examine your life. Are you taking full advantage of your salvation? Do you realize it is more than "fire insurance"? If you are at the crossroads of a decision, will you speak God's wisdom to the situation? Romans 10:10 says, "For with the heart man believeth unto righteousness; and with the mouth confession is made unto salvation." Salvation is for those who have been made righteous through Jesus Christ. The execution of your salvation is in your mouth. God's Word spoken through you confirms what is already yours and releases your faith for God to make it reality in your life. Doing so sends a message to the devil that you know who you are and that he can't block you from receiving what God has promised you as an inheritance.

SET YOURSELF UP FOR SUCCESS

Accepting God's salvation package is how you set yourself up for success. Confessing God's Word and acting on it establishes your steps and leads you to a path of success and abundance. If you haven't received Jesus as your Lord and Savior, now is the time for you to make that decision. Begin to speak the Word of God. Take it one step and one day at a time, and continue speaking His Word until you reach such a level of confidence in the Word that nothing can cause you to neglect your rights as a Believer.

Accepting salvation is the most important decision you'll ever make. It guarantees you'll spend eternity with God, and it empowers you to succeed in every area of your life. It will lead you to a destination of overflowing goodness and total-life prosperity. There are many people on their way to Heaven, but they aren't enjoying the journey. They may not be experiencing God's best in their lives for a number of reasons. The relationship you develop with God through His Son, Jesus, however, has the power to make your life on Earth enjoyable and fulfilling.

If you haven't developed a personal relationship with Jesus, the Anointed One, I invite you to do so today. God will meet you where you are. His love is unconditional and has nothing to do with how good or bad you think you are. When you invite Him into your heart, He'll smooth out the rough spots and set you free from your past. Make a decision, right now, to confess with your mouth that Jesus Christ is the Son of God and that He paid the price for your sins when He died on the cross. The Bible says that if you believe in your heart and say with your mouth that God raised Jesus from the dead, you will be saved (Romans 10:9). Make Him the final authority in your life, and consult Him on everything you do. Fellowship with Him through prayer and reading His Word.

God will meet you where you are. His love is unconditional and has nothing to do with how good or bad you think you are.

If you have opened your heart to Jesus today, welcome to the family of God! Angels are rejoicing over your decision (Luke 15:10) and right now in Heaven, your name has been written in the Lamb's Book of Life (Revelation 21:27). Praise God! You are now an heir of salvation and entitled to receive every covenant promise in the Bible.

Your decision to follow God's plan for your life, starting with salvation, is a life-changing moment. This marks only the beginning of your destiny with God!

Review Nuggets

Accepting Jesus as your Lord and Savior is the best decision you will ever make. Salvation is more than just being born again. It means *soteria*: wholeness, deliverance, victory, prosperity, health, and welfare. When you become born again, you take the first step toward reaching your divine destiny and achieving the total-life prosperity God has promised you in His Word. God desires to be reconciled with you and to be the final authority in your life. He wants to position you for greatness! Salvation is key to unlocking your destiny. Decide to live a life of wholeness today!

Foundation Scripture

I pray God your whole spirit and soul and body be preserved blameless unto the coming of our Lord Jesus Christ. Faithful is he that calleth you, who also will do it.

1 Thessalonians 5:23, 24

Practical Application

If you haven't accepted Jesus as your Lord and Savior, make a decision to do so today. If you confess your sins, God is faithful and just to forgive you and cleanse you of all unrighteousness (1 John 1:9).

Your salvation has benefits. Access your inheritance by examining areas in your life that need to be whole. Then activate salvation in those areas by speaking God's Word over them every day. Write down the results you experience for the next thirty days.

The Word—
God's Manual for Life

Have you ever wondered what your purpose in life is and what your future holds? We all want to make the most out of our lives and experience enjoyment and satisfaction while we're doing it. But how can we determine whether we will arrive at the "right" destination? Picture your life twenty years from now. Does your current lifestyle predict that you will be happy and fulfilled, or disappointed and frustrated? Think about it. What does your bank account look like? How much retirement money have you set aside? How much debt do you owe? What are you doing to improve your health and well-being? How is your family *really* doing? The answers to these questions may be an indication that a few changes need to be made.

If you are like most people, I'm sure you'd like to be happy, healthy, and financially independent twenty years from now, or today for that matter. If you want to know what you can do now to increase your chances of having the type of life you dream of, I have good news. First, you must make God's Word the foundation for your life. It makes all the difference in the world. Second, you must realize that God *wants* you to enjoy the good life. Third, you must be confident that the life you want is well within your reach.

Before God created you, He planned your future. That may sound hard to believe, but the Word of God proves it. Psalm 139:16 says that before you were even formed, God had already purposed all the days of your life! Isn't that amazing? He knew, approved, and chose *you* to accomplish a specific task. He also gave you talents and abilities that are uniquely designed to fit into His plan and propel you toward purposeful and abundant living.

YOUR GUIDE FOR LIVING

God's Word is His will, and it is only when you seek *His* plan that you can achieve the success and fulfillment you desire. His Word is foundational to success in this area. It is the roadmap that helps guide you to your divine destination. The simple truth is, the Bible is your manual for life. Without it, any path you take could very well lead to a dead end.

The Bible is your manual for life.

Second Timothy 3:16 says, "Every Scripture is God-breathed (given by His inspiration) and profitable for instruction" (AMP). For years, many people have debated the authenticity of the Bible and questioned whether it is really a divinely inspired message to humanity from God. Historians and scientists have tried to disprove its accuracy, but at the end of the day, none of their arguments hold water. Some argue that the Bible has changed through various stages of translation, but the discovery of the Dead Sea Scrolls in 1947 confirmed that modern translations are consistent with the earliest known manuscripts. Even the most recent scientific discoveries confirm the existence of many of the events, names, and places mentioned in Scripture.

Another popular argument is that the Bible is outdated and doesn't pertain to modern life. However, the Bible is still the *only* book that can be relied upon for truth and instruction concerning life. In it you will find the solution to every challenge you face. From Genesis to Revelation, its practical wisdom has proven to be timeless. For example, the book of Leviticus outlines dietary guidelines concerning foods that should and should not be eaten. If you compare the information to current medical reports, you will discover that some of the foods God told the Israelites not to eat are the same foods doctors and dieticians label "unhealthy." This is just one example of the Bible's relevance to our lives! In addition, Bible prophecy is being played out before our very eyes, as is evident by the turbulent times in which we live. War, chaos, and ungodliness are all around us.

Sadly, however, there are people who don't recognize the Bible's relevance to their everyday lives. They believe the miracles they've read about that occurred during biblical times, but they don't believe that God will perform the same miracles of healing, deliverance, and provision in their lives today. In fact, some believe that God will do more for others than He will for them. It is inconceivable for them to believe that God *wants* them to live the abundant life filled with His blessing. Instead, they believe the hard times they go through are God's way of teaching them a lesson.

The truth is, God has given us His Word as a directional guide for how to live. Before a person gives his life to Christ, he lives by the dictates of a system filled with wrong ideas, thoughts and beliefs. I call this system the world's system. It is the platform by which many of us were raised and trained. Until we go to Heaven, we must live in the world, but thank God we don't have to live by its standards.

When a person accepts Christ, his life is transformed and the Word of God becomes the catalyst for change. The transformation process is what is known as the "born-again experience." It is a decision to no longer think, act, or believe the same as before. It is also a wonderful opportunity to rid ourselves of the baggage, mistakes, and decisions of our past, so that we may live a new and better life.

The only way we can truly experience change is by renewing our minds to think in line with God and His Word. The Word is the foundation on which everything is established. Through this, we can create the life we want and fulfill God's purpose for our lives!

The way we think governs the way we live. Until we allow our hearts and minds to be renewed by God's Word, we will never completely fulfill our purpose. We are better able to identify the path that leads to our destination by allowing the Word of God to shape our thoughts. Just as a car manufacturer provides a manual of instruction for each car it makes, our Maker has provided written instructions for us as well. This is why it is so important that we make the Word of God the centerpiece of our lives. Our success in life depends on it.

GOD'S WORD LEADS TO
SUCCESS AND RECOVERY

Before you can reach your destination, you must become established in the truth of God's Word and understand the role it plays in your life. Now, what do I mean when I say you must be *established in the truth* of God's Word? I am saying you must be rooted and grounded in His Word. No matter what anyone says or what challenges may lie ahead, you must make a decision to trust God's promises.

You see, there are certain facts about our lives, and certain truths, that can be found only in God's Word. The fact may appear to be your reality, but the truth is what God says about your situation. For example, the *fact* may be that you just lost your job, but the *truth* is that God will supply all your needs (Philippians 4:19). Or the *fact* may be that you have an incurable disease. The *truth*, however, is that by the stripes of Jesus you are healed and made whole (Isaiah 53:5; 1 Peter 2:24). God's Word is what you rely on during difficult times, because what you believe ultimately dictates your outcome. Mark 11:23 says, "Truly I tell you, whoever says to this mountain, Be lifted up and thrown into the sea! and does not doubt at all in his heart but believes that what he says will take place, it will be done for him" (AMP). Believing and speaking God's promises is a vital action step to receiving God's promises.

After you practice this method of saying and believing God's Word and begin seeing results, you will be unmovable. You will look your situations square in the face and say, "I agree with God!" No matter what it looks like or sounds like, you will overcome every circumstance because you are established in the truth of God's Word. The Bible says in Ephesians 6:13, "Wherefore take unto you the whole armour of God, that ye may be able to withstand in the evil day, and having done all, to stand." I like how the Amplified Bible states it: "Therefore put on God's complete armor, that you may be able to resist and stand your ground on the evil day [of danger], and, having done all [the crisis demands], to stand [firmly in your place]." Likewise I say to you, stand until you get what you're standing there for.

Stand until you get what you're standing there for.

When you make God's Word, rather than the situations you face, your primary focus, everything will fall into place. By allowing the Word to guide your thoughts and actions, you will make significant progress in life and you will never go wrong. Even when you make a mistake, the Word on the inside of you will guide you back to the right path.

God's Word is the starting point for everything. In Genesis, God spoke words and the universe was created (Genesis 1:1–31). He has given us the same creative power that He possesses to speak things into existence (Proverbs 18:20, 21; Mark 11:23). Just as God's words created the world, His Word spoken from your mouth should also be the starting point for everything you do.

For example, if you're starting a new business, the first thing you should do is find specific Scriptures from the Word of God that you can stand on. Habakkuk 2:2 says, "And the Lord answered me and said, Write the vision and engrave it so plainly upon tablets that everyone who passes may [be able to] read [it easily and quickly] as he hastens by" (AMP).

Write the vision just as the Word of God recommends. Then share it with the right people so they may clearly understand your vision and help you fulfill it. God gives legs to the vision through people He assigns to assist you. Organize and develop a plan so that you can clearly present it to others who can help you turn it into reality.

God's Word is filled with promises to bless and empower His children. But none of His promises will work unless we do our part. Deuteronomy 28:1, 2 says, "If you will listen diligently to the voice of the Lord your God, being watchful to do all His commandments which I command you this day, the Lord your God will set you high above all the nations of the earth. And all these blessings shall come upon you and overtake you" (AMP). By learning to comply with God's Word, you can experience the good life God speaks about in Ephesians 2:10 when He says:

> For we are God's [own] handiwork (His workmanship), recreated in Christ Jesus, [born anew] that we may do those good works which God predestined (planned beforehand) for us [taking paths which He prepared ahead of time], that we should walk in them [living the good life which He prearranged and made ready for us to live]. (AMP)

Nothing in life just happens. The problems and challenges people face are often the result of their lack of knowledge concerning the Word of God. They don't know or understand God's perspective about certain things. Some reject His Word altogether. Yet there are others who recognize its value. They know what it says, but they choose to agree only with certain parts of it. Living this way is like taking half a pill rather than a whole one. There may be some benefit to consuming a portion of the medicine, but taking the whole dose would produce far better results.

Jesus made a remarkable statement in Matthew 4:4 when the devil tempted Him: "It is written, Man shall not live by bread alone, but by every word that proceedeth out of the mouth of God." Here Jesus makes clear that we should live by the Word. The Bible sustains you spiritually just as food sustains you physically.

You may be thinking right now, *What does all this talk about the Bible have to do with me finding my purpose and creating the life I want?* The answer is, *everything!* It is impossible to talk about success and destiny without emphasizing the absolute importance of God's Word and the foundational role it plays in your life. When you read, speak, and listen to God's Word daily, allowing it to saturate your heart, you create a solid foundation for success.

UNDERSTAND THE PROGRESSION

Your life's journey begins with the words you speak and hear, positive or negative. Words are powerful; they have the ability to reverse any situation. The best words I know can be found in God's Word. Believing what God says is vital, but speaking His Word is even more powerful.

Every decision you make in life has a direct impact on your future destination. Remember:

1. Revolutionize your words; they become your foundation.
2. Words produce thoughts.
3. Thoughts produce emotions.
4. Emotions produce decisions.
5. Decisions produce actions.
6. Actions produce habits.
7. Habits produce character.
8. Character produces destiny.

The choices you make in this progression will determine the type of life you will have. They determine whether your life will be mediocre, average, or extraordinary. You see, a person's background, educational, or financial status doesn't guarantee his destiny. Sure, all those things play a part, but what matters more is how a person lives. Our words, thoughts, and actions govern the choices we make.

The way you think today is a result of the words you've heard, said, and believed over time. Words are like seeds that produce after their own kind. For instance, if you plant apple seeds, you will harvest apples. If you plant corn, you will harvest corn. In the same way, Scriptures are also seeds; they will produce God's promises in your life. This same principle applies to your practical, everyday life. If you are sick and you consistently say, "With His stripes [I am] healed" (Isaiah 53:5), you plant seeds of healing in your heart, mind, and body that ultimately produce healing. Or if you're behind on your bills and you make the confession, "My God shall supply all [my] needs" (Philippians 4:19), you plant seeds for God's provision, and as a result, your needs are met.

Consider God's Word, then, as a bag of seeds. When these seeds are planted in your heart, you can literally create the future you desire. Meditating on a single Scripture until it impacts your thinking can turn your circumstances around. Even if you're already headed in a positive direction, putting God's Word to work in your life can only propel you forward. Joshua 1:8 says that by meditating on God's Word day and night, you make your way prosperous. God doesn't make you prosperous; meditating on His Word and applying it to your life makes you prosperous. When you spend quality time pondering the Word, and rolling it over in your mind until you fully understand it, you will gain the insight and wisdom you need to accomplish the things you desire.

> *When you spend quality time pondering the Word, and rolling it over in your mind until you fully understand it, you will gain the insight and wisdom you need to accomplish the things you desire.*

Renewing your mind with the Word of God is a daily practice. It is not something that happens overnight. It requires diligence and consistency on your part. Begin by choosing a time of day that is good for you. Get into God's presence by tuning out the world around you. Turn off the television. Move to a room away from your family, and avoid distractions. Talk to Him; wait for His response with earnest expectation. Take the time to study His Word and apply it to your life. The time you spend with God will reshape your thinking about everything—your relationships, finances, and aspirations. Like food, let it be the one thing you consume on a regular basis. To neglect time spent with God is to delay the promises you expect to receive.

THE MISSING ELEMENT

Many people feel there is something missing in their lives. They know what they want out of life, but they don't know what to do to achieve their goals. They yearn for fulfillment and satisfaction. They search for it in people, promotions, and get-rich-quick schemes. Yet for some, years go by and they have little to show in the way of progress.

God's Word provides the building blocks for everything we desire. It is *our* responsibility to use what He has given us. A close relationship with Him, developed through the study and application of His Word, is often the missing element. Some people find it hard to believe that they can positively affect the situations in their lives by reading and quoting Scriptures. However, the truth is, it works! I've seen it work time and time again in my own life. My wife, Taffi, and I used this very method to get out of debt. We used it again to build our church, debt-free. We've used it where our children are concerned, and we've never seen it fail.

If you've struggled to achieve your goals or if you've experienced a setback that you're still trying to overcome, you don't have to suffer any longer. Many Believers deny themselves the good life that has already been reserved and freely given to them by God. He doesn't want you to struggle. He wants you to be completely sufficient in everything and lacking nothing.

In John 10:10 Jesus says, "The thief comes only in order to steal and kill and destroy. I came that they may have and enjoy life, and have it in abundance (to the full, till it overflows)" (AMP). God never planned for you to lack anything. He is a good God and wants to do you good and make you happy! But the "thief," who is the devil, seeks to do you harm.

Now, let's go back to the question I asked at the beginning of this chapter: *What does the future hold for you?* Based on God's promises, your answer should be, without question, abundant life, great health and longevity, peace of mind, happiness, and financial prosperity! Living a life in the overflow of God's blessings is His will for you. His promises are intended for your benefit and enjoyment, but they won't just magically appear. You, too, have a role to play. The keys below will help:

1. Make the Word of God your foundation in life.

2. Spend time reading and meditating on His Word daily.

3. Find Scriptures (seeds) about the things you desire or want to change.

4. Plant the seeds in your heart by consistently reciting them.

Your mission in life is to choose the path that leads to the destination God has already prepared for you. There is a unique purpose for your life, and God's Word is the key that will unlock your destiny and allow it to unfold. Make a decision today to give God and His Word the highest position in your life—you won't regret it!

Review Nuggets

Making the Word of God your foundation in life is a must. God *wants* you to enjoy the good life. You must have confidence in this fact—it makes all the difference in the world. The Bible is your manual for life. Its messages are entirely true and contain practical wisdom for daily living.

Your thoughts are influenced by the words you speak and believe. Your emotions, decisions, actions, habits, and character follow suit. In the end, your character determines your destination!

Foundation Scripture

For we are God's [own] handiwork (His workmanship), recreated in Christ Jesus, [born anew] that we may do those good works which God predestined (planned beforehand) for us [taking paths which He prepared ahead of time], that we should walk in them [living the good life which He prearranged and made ready for us to live].

Ephesians 2:10 (AMP)

Practical Application

Choose three areas in your life that you would like to change or improve. Find a concordance or use an online Bible resource to locate Scriptures on each subject. For example, if you need a house, look up words like *house* or *land*. If you need healing, look up *healed, healing,* and *health*. Once you've found a few Scriptures on each subject, begin reciting your favorites over and over again for the next twenty-one days. Write down your testimonies in a notebook or journal as they occur. Give your book a special name and refer to it often to stay encouraged. God is faithful!

The Battle
of Words

Have you ever played chess? In this challenging competition, the object of the game is to capture your opponent's most valuable piece—the king. As you advance across the board, you strategically maneuver through your opponent's tactics without being captured. However, if the opponent breaks through your line of defense and secures *your* king, you lose the game.

I like to think of life in the same way. You have an enemy who is trying to gain control of your most valuable asset—your mind. Satan uses words to try to influence you to go against God's Word, and if you yield to his attempts, he will succeed in defeating you in the game of life. Your job is to employ a strategy that will keep him out of your mind, and ultimately out of your heart. To defeat him, you must rely on the strategy found in God's Word.

Every day Satan launches multiple attacks against you. He wants to influence your thinking in order to maneuver you away from the path in which God is directing you. He uses circumstances, people, and even your past to get you off track. Before you know it, you find yourself someplace you didn't intend to be—discouraged, stressed, and confused.

In the battle of words, it's God's Word versus Satan's words. The enemy's objective is to plant *his* words in your mind so that he can bring *his* will to pass in your life. Although it may seem appealing and harmless at first, his plan leads to a destination of trouble, disappointment, and defeat. He wants to destroy God's plan for your life—the good life God promised you in Ephesians 2:10 (AMP). God wants you to be free from every form of oppression, including sickness, debt, lack, and failure. This freedom is the life Jesus purchased for you when He died on the cross and rose again.

> *God wants you to be free from every form of oppression,*
> *including sickness, debt, lack, and failure.*

GOD'S ORIGINAL PLAN

To give you a clearer picture of the type of life God intends for you to enjoy, let's revisit the Garden of Eden, *before* sin entered the picture. Can you imagine having everything you need and desire right at your fingertips—no bills, no credit or employment applications, no "waiting until the time is right," and no problems? Imagine a life without crime, war, divorce, sickness, poverty, pollution, or death. Just think of it: communing with God in person daily, without ever waiting to have a prayer answered. Now that's the good life!

The Bible says that the Garden of Eden was rich with gold and other natural metals (Genesis 2:11, 12). To me, the word *Eden* means "voluptuous living," because everything you need is right there at your fingertips. This is the type of lifestyle that Adam and Eve experienced before they sinned. It was like a part of heaven on the earth!

This was God's design for our lives. Sin, death, disaster, and economic shortage were *never* part of His plan. No, God's original intent was for us to rule the Earth just as He rules Heaven. In the book of Genesis, God gave man dominion, full charge, and ownership over everything He created!

To overturn God's plan, Satan launched an attack in the Garden that changed the course of history. He introduced sin into the world by way of temptation. His arsenal? Words! By planting a seed of doubt in Eve's mind, Satan prompted her to question God and doubt His promises. The more Eve listened to the enemy's lies, the more curious she became.

In her temptation, she influenced Adam's thinking. His thinking influenced his actions, and he followed her into sin. His decision changed his destination. Through one simple act of disobedience, Adam and Eve gave up the good life God had freely given them, in exchange for what appeared to be more.

In our own lives we have a tendency to do the same thing. We think the grass will be greener on the other side. Then, against our better judgment, and all the warning signs God places before us, we detour from the path that leads to His best as we search for what *appears* to be greater.

What has the devil been suggesting to you lately? What thoughts is he trying to plant in your heart right now to sabotage God's plan for you? The sooner you identify the enemy's tactics, the closer you will be to getting rid of them and moving forward in your destiny. The power of suggestion is a divisive tool the enemy uses to lead us away from our divine destination. He's like a used-car salesman. He polishes up what he knows will capture our attention and tells us all about its benefits, and why it's so much better than what we already have, until we're finally convinced that buying into his idea is the best thing that could ever happen.

THE GARDEN IN YOUR HEART

Just as the Garden of Eden was Adam and Eve's place of abundant supply and voluptuous living, so is the heart of man. Depending on what you plant, the heart is soil that has the potential to create great harvest. The Word of God is like a bag of seeds. When planted, God's promises will produce the desired result. To plant the Word in your heart, you must read it, speak it, and meditate on it daily. God's Word will change your life! By planting it in your heart, you cultivate it to produce the fruit of His promises. Reading, meditating on, and speaking God's Word is the way to get it into the soil of your heart. This will bring into existence the very things you desire.

The heart is soil that has the potential to create great harvest.

Remember, though, that in the same way that you plant seeds of faith and belief in your heart, it is also possible to plant seeds of doubt and unbelief. By entertaining Satan's lies, you can create a life of lack, filled with pressures and failed expectations. His goal is to get you off course. When you yield to his temptation to go against God's Word, you will be fully engulfed in his plan, making it difficult—although not impossible—to get out.

We live in a word-created, word-controlled environment. Words are spiritual containers that carry faith or fear, blessing or cursing. When you speak words, they begin to take shape in the spirit realm, then later in the natural realm. For example, you might say, "I'm broke, and I don't think I'll ever get out of debt." If you say that, then that's exactly what you'll have. Or you could choose to say, "I don't have the money to buy everything I want and need right now, but my God shall supply all my needs, and by faith, I will be out of debt soon!" You have what you say, so it is wise to choose words carefully. The words you speak, either positive or negative, are seeds that will produce an outcome.

The Word of God is the *only* trustworthy source of words. It is the incorruptible seed that *never* fails. God's Word always produces a harvest. Every word you speak is a seed, but God's Word is the seed that leads to satisfaction and wholeness.

God used words to set the world into motion. He created every living thing, including mankind, by speaking words of faith. Genesis 1:1–31 describes how God created the Heavens and the Earth and every living thing. The process of creation began with, "God said," and then, "God saw what He had made." The Bible says that when God created man, He breathed the breath of life into him. What this actually means is that God spoke to the clay-like figure of a man that He created from the ground and breathed His Spirit into him, and man *became* a living soul (Genesis 2:7).

This same creative ability that God possesses to speak things into existence is also within you! He has given you full authority over everything. You were created in His image, and you must be confident in the power and ability He has given you. The Word of God says you shall have what you say (Mark 11:23). God has given you the right to decree a thing, and the Word says it *shall* be done unto you (Job 22:28)!

You have probably heard the phrase, "You hold the keys to your destiny." This is absolutely true. The keys are the words you speak. Now that you know the power of words, you don't have to be a victim of situations and circumstances another day! Your social or economic status doesn't determine your success or failure in life; that is determined by the words you believe and speak. When you understand the power of speaking God's Word, you won't live an average or mediocre life. You'll live an extraordinary life!

> *You don't have to be a victim of situations*
> *and circumstances another day!*

TWO SYSTEMS OF INFLUENCE

All it takes is one flip of the television channel or a glance at newspaper headlines to see that the world we live in today is in a state of chaos and uncertainty. Sure, there have been turbulent times throughout the history of the world, but there is no question in my mind that we are now living in the End Times. Satan knows his time is short, and he is turning up the heat. Violence, perversion, war, and fear are on the rise like never before. There is a battle going on for the souls of men, a battle between the Kingdom of God and the kingdom of darkness.

There are no in-betweens and no exceptions: you belong to either the Kingdom of God or the kingdom of darkness, and both sides are controlled by words. The words of God's Kingdom come from God and carry faith, love, life, peace, and blessing. The *blessing* is an empowerment to prosper or excel. The world's system, on the other hand, is dominated by words of the kingdom of darkness, ruled by Satan. It produces doubt, fear, poverty, sickness, death and the curse. The *curse* is "an empowerment to fail." According to Colossians 1:13, Believers have been translated out of the kingdom of darkness and into the Kingdom of God. It is our job, then, to do everything we can to resist the enemy's suggestions.

When a person is born again, everything becomes new. God offers a

new language—the language of faith! It is the Believer's responsibility
to study the Word of God, gain understanding of how to apply it to his
life, and plant seeds of God's Word in his heart. Likewise, when seeds
are planted in the soil of your heart, you will be responsive to God, and
a great harvest *will* come. The type of crop you harvest is determined
by the type of seeds you sow—either word-seeds from God's Word, or
word-seeds from Satan.

Now that you know it is Satan's plan to tempt you daily, you must
stay alert. Temptation is nothing more than pressure applied to your
thinking. The enemy usually tries to tempt us with things we like and
enjoy. He will also tempt us with things we've walked away from: maybe
a bad relationship, drugs, gambling, or stealing. When Satan tempts us,
we must remind ourselves that we're on God's team and the battle has
already been won. God is interested not in where we've been, but where
we're going. He is willing to forgive you the moment you repent, no
matter what you've said or done in the past.

> *We must remind ourselves that we're on God's*
> *team and the battle has already been won.*

Contrary to what you may think, you can't fight thoughts of temptation with "good thoughts." The Word says that the weapons of warfare
are not carnal (2 Corinthians 10:4). In other words, it's not the people
or circumstances in your life that you're up against; it is the enemy's
spirit operating through those people and situations. Simply put, the
only way to ward off Satan's temptations and stop them from pro-
gressing to full-blown action is to cast them down with God's Word
(2 Corinthians 10:5). That means that when Satan tries to plant the
wrong seed in your heart, you must *immediately* speak the Word of God
out loud. Doing this repeatedly will cast the thought down and help
you guard the soil of your heart.

You can't afford to allow opposing thoughts to take root in your
mind and get into your heart. Your heart fosters the growth of whatever
you plant in it. Make sure that the seeds you plant originate from God,
not Satan.

SAY IT AND SEE IT,
PLANT IT AND GROW IT

Hearing and seeing words are two ways in which word-seeds can get into your heart, but speaking them is the most powerful method. God has given you the creative ability to speak things into existence. Whatever you say has the potential to become a reality. If you are saying the wrong things—words that oppose the Bible—you *will* see them come to pass. Repent of them and begin setting your course with positive, faith-filled words.

It is critical that you choose your words carefully and refrain from speaking *idle* words (words that are empty or void of faith). Speaking idle words actually deceives your heart! For example, using words associated with death has become the norm in everyday conversation. It is not uncommon to hear people say things like, "That tickled me to death," or, "I hate brussels sprouts." Most people may not really believe that the more they declare their hatred for something, the more they will despise it, so they continue to use such phrases. But your heart is programmed to produce what is planted in it, and when you constantly speak words that you don't believe, you train yourself in doubt and unbelief. Those words won't bring forth a positive result.

As you become a spiritual "farmer" of God's Word, daily planting, cultivating, and guarding your soil, you will see great results. When you plant the Word of God in your heart by keeping it before your eyes, hearing it, and confessing it with your mouth, even in the face of negative circumstances, you position yourself for a positive outcome.

As you become a spiritual "farmer" of God's Word, daily planting, cultivating, and guarding your soil, you will see great results.

GUARD YOUR GARDEN

I remember watching the news on a particular day and hearing a scientist say something to this effect: "Our worst fears are going to come true. The bird flu is coming, and it's going to kill millions of people. We are very worried and fear that soon, the bird flu will become a reality." Although the bird flu may be a legitimate threat, this individual conveyed fear and panic with his words. Undoubtedly, many people heard him and were frightened.

This is just one example of how negative reports can impact our lives. Of course we need to know about potential epidemics and other newsworthy concerns, but I wouldn't recommend watching the twenty-four-hour news channel all the time, or reading the bad reports in the newspapers every day with your breakfast. Constantly feeding your spirit fear-based words will inevitably produce fear in your life. At that point, all Satan has to do is get you to speak them. Then he will have an open door to bring to pass what you fear the most (Job 3:25).

In the example mentioned above, the scientist let his personal fears determine the words he spoke. There was no concrete evidence that the disease was killing millions of people, or that it would. What words have you heard through the media that have planted seeds of doubt, fear, and unbelief?

Music is another area that must be carefully monitored when it comes to the battle of words. Satan is subtle. He can easily plant his message in your heart through popular music. This is perhaps one of the most powerful and dangerous tools he uses, because once a song is in your mind, all it takes is for you to sing it for it to penetrate your heart.

Nearly everyone is exposed to music that influences their words and thoughts. Unfortunately, many of the hit songs today promote violence, sex, and a lifestyle of perversion. Think about the impact that these words can have on children, teenagers, and adults. You may be saying, "But, Brother Dollar, it's only a song!" That's just what the enemy would like you to think. But the sad truth is that people are seriously affected by the words they receive into their hearts for the sake of entertainment.

Have you ever listened to a sad love song and begun feeling sad? Or if you were going through relationship trouble, did you play songs that reinforced your feelings? Do you ever hear songs now that take you back to another time and place? Certain songs can remind you of a person, time, or activity from your past. Other songs can spark your imagination and make you visualize things that have yet to happen. It may not seem like a big deal at the time, but once you saturate your mind and heart with certain themes, you'll find it difficult to think about anything else!

Songs filled with violence have the potential to take the mind in a terrible direction. Even if a person doesn't commit a crime, the words of a particular song can still plant negative seeds that lead to destruction. If teens sow enough violence into their hearts through this type of music, they will eventually show signs of the type of behavior the music describes.

I remember popular songs like "Fire" by the Ohio Players and "Mary Jane" by Rick James. As I think back to the lyrics, they were quite negative, yet impactful. As I sang those songs, I had no idea that I was planting seeds of lust deep in my heart. What's worse is that sometimes we sing songs even though we really don't agree with the words. They just sound good or we like the beat.

You may be thinking, *Am I supposed to stop listening to music?* Proverbs 4:23 says to keep your heart with all diligence because the issues of your life flow out of it. While I am not suggesting that you stop listening to music, I do recommend that you take inventory of your favorite music and carefully examine the lyrics. Guard your heart, and make sure the music you listen to contains lyrics that feed your spirit with words that are in line with God's Word.

Above all, remember that the battle of words continues. Whose message will you listen to—God's or the enemy's?

Review Nuggets

The Word of God is a bag of seeds. Seeds will produce a harvest in your life, either good or bad. The Word of God is *the* seed you need to plant in your heart to grow success, love, wealth, and healing. The primary battle that every Believer faces is the battle of words. By focusing on God's Word, you guard the soil of your heart from Satan's suggestions.

In the same way that God created the world by speaking it into existence, you must also use your mouth to speak those things that you desire. When you do, you become a co-creator with Him and are empowered to do all things!

Foundation Scripture

He taught me and said to me, Let your heart hold fast my words; keep my commandments and live.

Proverbs 4:4 (AMP)

Practical Application

Ridding yourself of negative thoughts takes discipline. For the next twenty-one days, pay close attention to thoughts that oppose the Word of God. Find Scriptures that dispute these thoughts, and write each one on a 3×5 index card. Carry the cards with you and begin memorizing them. Every time you have an opposing thought, take out your card and read the Scripture. Find a quiet place where you can be alone, and recite the Scripture until you believe it without a doubt.

Word Power

Words have profound power. You can literally feel it when someone speaks harshly or negatively to you. It's as though the area of your brain that controls your speech is connected to every nerve in your body! Similarly, God's Word brings healing to your physical body, peace to your mind, and nourishment to your soul (Proverbs 4:20–22). Words have power!

> *God's Word brings healing to your physical body, peace*
> *to your mind, and nourishment to your soul.*

We have established that there are two systems of operation on Earth—God's system and the world's system. Each is governed by words. The words you speak will connect you to either the rewards or the consequences of one of these systems. Words have the power to accelerate or delay your progress altogether. Therefore we must train ourselves to be more selective in our choice of words.

I know *training* is a dirty word for some people, but just as you were trained to speak the world's language, you must retrain yourself to speak God's language. Sometimes when I hear my teens talk, I don't know what they're saying. I hear young men greeting each other at the mall and saying things like, "What's up, dog!" I'm thinking, "Did he just call that guy an animal?" I'm sure it was the same way for my parents when I was growing up. Rather than saying we were dating someone, we'd say, "We go together." "Go where together?" was likely my parents' response.

Even in business, we use special terminology to relate to one another. Someone may say, "I've got a part-time gig." That means that he or she has a part-time job. We "surf the net," we "chat" online, and we "do" lunch. We adapt to the environment we're in, and amazingly, we somehow understand each other.

There's nothing wrong with using this type of terminology. It helps us relate to one another. However, when we use faithless, negative words in our communication, we trap ourselves needlessly. Let's say you're looking for a new job and someone asks you how the final interview went. You respond, "Well, I may not have the same experience as the other guy they're considering, but I hope I get the job." Chances are, you won't. It would be better to say, "It went well. My experience proved to be beneficial in the conversation, and I look forward to learning new aspects of the job. I expect a callback any day."

Allowing God's Word to govern the words you speak doesn't mean that you have to become spiritually deep. Some Christians feel that they have to include ten Scriptures and clichés in their response to every simple question. Here's an example of what I mean: "How are you today, ma'am?" "Oh, Brother Dollar, I'm highly favored of the Lord. I have on the breastplate of righteousness. I'm filled with the Spirit. No weapon formed against me shall prosper, and I'm just blessed!" By the time she says all that, I'm afraid to ask how the kids are doing and whether she's still looking for a new house.

Now, let me add balance to this. It's perfectly okay to respond with faith-filled words. In fact, I encourage it, but at the appropriate time. If someone asks you to pray at Thanksgiving dinner, that's not the time to begin speaking in tongues or running down your list of confessions. Simply say the prayer and eat. Praying in tongues isn't going to make the food more pure or delicious. There's no accelerated progress by praying in tongues. On the other hand, if you're sick and someone asks how you're feeling, standing on your faith will accelerate your healing: "I'm feeling a little under the weather, but by faith I'm healed." Do you see the difference?

I spent a lot of time giving you those scenarios because I want you to understand my heart on this matter. Training yourself to speak faith-filled words is vital. Whether it is during your prayer time, while driving in your car, or in a conversation at work, invite God in. Make a conscious effort to make progress in this area every day. If you're still using curse words, calling your children names, or throwing out idle phrases like, "I'm broke," don't beat yourself up. Instead, make the change. Ridding yourself of negative speech won't happen overnight, but it will happen and it will make a difference. Feel free to correct yourself right in the middle of saying or thinking things that are not in line with the Word. It will help you to develop a Word-consciousness.

Remember, words are seeds. Every time you speak, you are planting seeds in your heart and setting events in motion. Don't just say whatever you want without using wisdom and discretion. Speak wisely, and experience a continuous flow of God's blessing.

Every time you speak, you are planting seeds in your heart and setting events in motion.

REVERSE THE DAMAGE

You may be a victim of years of speaking wrong words or having the wrong types of words spoken to or about you. Maybe you grew up in a broken home, with parents and siblings who verbally abused you. Perhaps no one ever told you about the power of words, and you didn't know any better. That all ends today. You now have the tools and resources you need to begin reversing the damage negative words have caused in your life. Start speaking your divine destiny into existence.

For years, people have talked about the power of positive words. Even those in secular circles tout the impact words have on a person's psyche and outcome in life. It's not just a cliché that words are powerful—it's a biblical truth! The Bible plainly says, "Death and life are in the power of the tongue" (Proverbs 18:21). Once you master your words, you can change your present and future circumstances.

Reversing damage that has been sustained by negative words begins with a quality decision to change. You must accept the fact that Satan wants to rob you of your destiny through subtle thought injections. It's what he did in the Garden of Eden with Adam and Eve, and it is the same thing he is doing today. He speaks words that oppose God's Word to affect your thinking, your emotions, and ultimately your decisions.

If you have accepted the negative words that have been spoken to or about you, you can turn the results around today. Get in the Word of God and believe what He has to say about you. Get a concordance, and take time to read your Bible *every day*. There are plenty of study resources available. Even more exciting is the assurance of knowing that whatever issues you may be facing right now, there is a specific Scripture related to that issue. God has written you sixty-six love letters designed to steer you on the road to success and help prevent and reverse the damaging effects of Satan's suggestions on your mind. Discover these practical truths by getting into the Word.

Once you find out what God has to say about a particular issue or situation, you've got to become established in His truth. This is accomplished by meditating on the Word until it becomes reality. The truth of God's Word has to become more real to you than the things you see with your natural eye. You are inundated with negative words, images, and suggestions every day. In order to combat these forces, you need to spend more time with God than you do with anything else.

Set aside time in your day to read and meditate on the Word of God. Speak the Scriptures aloud concerning your situation until you become grounded in the truth. That will create a force field of God's protection around you that the devil won't be able to penetrate.

*Speak the Scriptures aloud concerning your situation
until you become grounded in the truth.*

If you've spoken a lot of negative words, begin the process of reversal today. This is a key to turning your future around. As you begin practicing God's presence by talking to Him daily and keeping His Word at the forefront of your mind, you will develop a Word-consciousness. When you hear or say something that opposes the Word of God, you will immediately be able to discern it and replace it with a faith-filled thought. The Holy Spirit will bring Scriptures you've planted in your heart to your remembrance the moment you need them.

AVOID THE SINS OF THE MOUTH

Besides knowing the *right* words to speak, you also need to be aware of the sins that you may be committing with your mouth so that you can avoid reaping the wrong harvest. When you know the type of speech that offends God and blocks His power from operating in your life, you will make an extra effort to keep your conversations in line with His Word.

It's amazing that the Bible contains so many Scriptures about the dangers of using words in the wrong way. The Word is filled with teachings on words that will hinder God and actually bring a curse into a person's life. Gossiping, complaining, lying, cursing, making fun of others, speaking idle words, and causing strife are all things we must guard ourselves against. Opening yourself up to them will stop your progress and block the blessings of God in your life.

According to Numbers 11, the children of Israel suffered because of their constant murmuring and complaining in the desert. Like them, we have opportunities to complain. But no matter how hard things may be, or what you may be going through, it's important to maintain an attitude of praise and thanksgiving for what God has *already* done in your life.

There is much value in the Golden Rule: "Do unto others as you would have them do unto you" (see also Matthew 7:12). Make sure that you speak words that are in line with God's Word. In Matthew 12:37, Jesus says, "For by thy words thou shalt be justified, and by thy words thou shalt be condemned." What you say *will* come back to you, to add either the blessing or the curse to your life, so think before you speak. If you set the wrong words into motion, cancel them immediately! Repent, and replace those negative words with positive words of faith.

SPEAK OUT OF AN ESTABLISHED HEART

God created human beings to function like Him on Earth. Since He is a Creator who uses words as building blocks, He expects you and me to operate the same way. If you give more thought to problems than solutions, your heart will be established in what currently exists, rather than in the faith of what *can* exist. To maximize God's power in your life, you must maximize the power He has already given you through words.

Jesus is our example. Part of His mission was to show us how to use the authority God has given us. We have the potential to do everything Jesus did and more with the words we speak (John 14:12). Through words, Jesus did the miraculous. He turned water into wine, and five loaves of bread and two fish into a fish dinner with an abundance of leftovers. He healed the sick and raised the dead. How? By establishing His heart in God's Word. The Scriptures were an integral part of who He was.

Part of how Jesus established His heart in God's Word was by meditating on them. "Meditation" means saying and thinking a thing over and over until it becomes embedded in your heart. It is more than just casually reading over Bible verses. It isn't sitting in a cross-legged position on the floor with your eyes closed as you chant out loud. It means pondering the Scriptures and turning them over in your mind until you squeeze every bit of revelation and understanding out of them.

Joshua 1:8 is a foundational Scripture that really speaks of the power of biblical meditation. It says, "This book of the law shall not depart out of thy mouth; but thou shalt meditate therein day and night, that thou mayest observe to do according to all that is written therein: for then thou shalt make thy way prosperous, and then thou shalt have good success." Only when your heart is full of the Word and has no doubt and unbelief will you be able to speak words of faith and create the reality you desire.

> *Only when your heart is full of the Word and has no doubt and unbelief will you be able to speak words of faith and create the reality you desire.*

Jesus wasn't a magician who used special tricks and stunts to heal people and raise the dead. No. He understood His authority, and when He spoke He got results. Jesus' words were full of faith and love. When He gave a command or spoke the truth of God's Word, situations and circumstances changed instantly. You possess the potential to experience the same results. In fact, Jesus said that you have the ability to do even more: "Greater works than these shall he do" (John 14:12). This supernatural ability to do greater works is a result of meditating on God's Word, believing it, and applying it. That's when God's super ability overtakes your natural ability and allows you to perform the supernatural.

If you'll apply these principles and establish your heart in God's Word, it won't be long before you'll notice a change in the way you live. You'll become especially mindful of the things you say. You'll also begin to take notice of the words you hear. When someone says, "This heat is killing me," you'll notice. Or when a complaining coworker starts spouting off about how terrible the boss is, you'll be less interested in getting involved in the conversation. The positive things you say about your job and your refusal to get involved in your coworker's complaining may, in fact, surprise him. It will not only begin to change his perception of you, it will also earn you a new level of respect.

Some may react and accuse you of being *deep* or taking this word-thing too far. But don't worry about what others may say because you're working on something! They'll be wondering how you suddenly began making achievements and experiencing greater success at work, while they remain stuck in the same position.

As you build the habit of speaking God's Word and releasing His power consistently, you'll move closer to your desired destination.

God's Word is true. Regardless of what you experience or the challenges you may see around you, hold on to His promises. Keep speaking the Word, no matter what. You will see results! Speak the Word when you're in pain—don't change your words to match any negative diagnosis the doctor may give you. Don't reinforce sickness and disease by caving in, quitting, or announcing the doctor's report to others. Announce to yourself, and to others, that you are healed!

At times it may appear you are losing the fight against whatever ails you, but in the long run, the power of your words will determine whether you win or lose the battle. Your children may need clothes and shoes, the rent may be due, and your bank account may be in the red, but if you keep reminding yourself of God's promise of provision, protection, and wholeness, your physical surroundings will begin to mirror those promises.

> *In the long run, the power of your words will*
> *determine whether you win or lose the battle.*

I know it's challenging when a negative report is looming over your head and it seems like all hope is lost, but when you speak what you see rather than what you want to see, you hinder your progress. A few years ago, my doctor delivered some startling news to me: he diagnosed me with prostate cancer. I already knew that Jesus paid the price for my healing, and I trusted God for divine health, but I was in for a battle, and I knew what I had to do in order to win it.

I told my wife, Taffi, what the doctor had said. Despite how we felt at the time, we made a decision to trust God where my healing was concerned. We decided that we would not broadcast the doctor's diagnosis to the people around us. Instead, we began to saturate ourselves in the Word of God. I found every Scripture that pertained to healing and began reading them day and night. I shut out everything else—television, phone calls, and the doubt and fear that tried to overtake my mind. Instead, I concentrated on receiving my healing through the power of God's Word. I read the Bible and books on healing. I repeated Scriptures about healing. I even watched and listened to tapes about healing. I kept them playing at work, in my car, and at home, all day long. My life was on the line, and it was imperative that my thoughts line up with God's Word.

Over the course of a few days, my faith in God's healing power increased. Taffi and I read Scriptures aloud from the time I received the doctor's report until the time I visited him again. This time his diagnosis was different. The test results indicated that the cancer was completely gone!

Speaking the Word works—and not just for healing. It will work in every circumstance you can imagine. Suppose you have challenges in your finances and you desire God's help. The first step toward activating His blessing in your finances is to speak what He has already said in His Word. The Bible says that God takes pleasure in the prosperity of His servants (Psalm 35:27). It also says that He will supply all your needs according to His riches in glory (Philippians 4:19). The more you know from the Word, the more faith you will have to get the results you desire.

Although using words to change your life requires discipline and patience, it's worth the effort. You'll see results sooner than you think! There are many trendy success strategies on the market today, but if you want enduring happiness and satisfaction in your life, employ God's Word. Let it work for you. Allow it to infiltrate your heart and create the life of your dreams. If you believe it, you've already begun to receive it!

*If you want enduring happiness and satisfaction
in your life, employ God's Word.*

Review Nuggets

It takes a carefully crafted plan to implement change in any area of your life. The desire to change your words is only one part of the process of making God's Word your foundation. Now that you've learned the importance of words and how they affect your heart, it's up to you to change your words by monitoring them constantly. Choose wholesome entertainment with positive messages void of explicit content. When others speak negative words to or about you, refuse to let them take root in your heart. Overcome negativity by believing what God says about you in His Word.

Speaking God's Word in the midst of bad circumstances is not *lying* or denying reality. When we speak what God has already spoken, we speak truth. Facts indicate temporary circumstances and are subject to change. God's Word is the *truth*, and it endures forever. While God's Word contains truths that you may not yet see, trust that you will. Changing the way you speak, the words you hear, and the images you see are very important steps to reaching your destiny in life. You will achieve God's perfect plan when you follow His blueprint. Frame your world with your words!

Foundation Scripture

Death and life are in the power of the tongue: and they that love it shall eat the fruit thereof.

Proverbs 18:21

Practical Application

Whatever your desires may be, the path to achieving your goals begins with your words. Utilize the power God has given you to create your future. Complete the following sentence and speak it aloud: "The one thing I want most out of life is _____." You don't have to narrow it down to one thing. Use your journal to make a list of the things you'd like to have or experience. Then find Scriptures to support each one, and begin confessing the things you desire daily. Try this for the next twenty-one days, and continue for as long as it takes. Naturally, we sometimes want things that don't agree with God's plan for our lives, but as you study His Word, He will point you in the right direction and place *His* desires in your heart. Cooperate with Him and allow your thoughts to line up with His plan for your life!

Make the Word-Thought Connection

What would you do if you were sitting in your home one Saturday morning and, all of a sudden, a delivery guy from a local bakery knocked on your front door to deliver a basket of freshly baked Danish? It would probably be a welcomed surprise, right? Even if you didn't know who the pastries came from, you'd probably sign for them with little or no reservation and begin reading the card just as you took your first bite. Now, what if someone attempted to deliver you a huge basket of rattlesnakes? Would you have the same reaction? I doubt it. You'd probably yell, "No way!" and slam the door.

A good friend of mine shared this analogy with me one day as we were discussing the subject of thoughts. I'll never forget it. He explained to me that, while we cannot stop certain thoughts from crossing our minds, we can choose whether we will accept them. Accepting every thought that crosses your mind is like accepting every basket that shows up at your door, even if it's a basket of rattlesnakes.

The great thing is, God has given each of us the ability to make our own choices. Once a word is spoken, we must make the choice to either receive or disregard it. It doesn't matter who's sending the message— a friend, an enemy, God, or Satan—*you* determine whether you will accept or reject it. Whatever you give attention to is what you will ultimately act on. This is why it is so important that you learn to distinguish the difference between God's Word and Satan's words.

*Once a word is spoken, we must make the
choice to either receive or disregard it.*

Reading the Bible and being in fellowship with the Father daily are key in making this determination. It's like spending time with someone. You begin to develop a relationship with that person, and after a while, you know the things he would and would not say. It's the same way with God. When Satan shows up to challenge you by saying, "Did God really say . . . ?" you will know with certainty that it is not God who is speaking. Once you identify a thought that opposes God's Word, recognize quickly that it is a message from the enemy, and reject it.

The Bible provides several examples of how words can influence a person's thoughts and actions to the point where they move out of the will of God. In this particular example, taken from Genesis 11:3–6, the people decided to build a tower to Heaven:

And they said one to another, Go to, let us make brick, and burn them thoroughly. And they had brick for stone, and slime had they for morter. And they said, Go to, let us build us a city and a tower, whose top may reach unto heaven; and let us make us a name, lest we be scattered abroad upon the face of the whole earth. And the LORD came down to see the city and the tower, which the children of men builded. And the LORD said, Behold, the people is one, and they have all one language; and this they begin to do: and now nothing will be restrained from them, which they have imagined to do.

This passage of Scripture demonstrates the power of words. Through their words, the people *said* they would build a tower to Heaven. After they spoke it, they began to envision themselves doing it. Then they responded with a corresponding action and set out to make it happen. You see, their thoughts led them to take action. God knew the power of their words and thoughts and interrupted their plans to keep them from destroying themselves.

If you allow negative words to linger in your mind and take root in your heart, they will influence the actions you take. It's just that simple. Someone once told me something that I'll never forget: You can't stop the birds from flying over your head, but you can keep them from building a nest in your hair. The same is true of your thoughts. You can't always control the thoughts that come to mind, but you can keep them from lingering and hindering your progress.

HOW TO TAME YOUR THOUGHTS WITH THE WORD

Using words to tame your thinking is a habit every Believer should develop. As the enemy increases his attacks in these last days, it is necessary that you know how to combat his assaults on your thinking. You must become a vigilant custodian over your thought life and allow the Word of God to be the guardian of your mind.

I often use the exercise I'm about to share with you to help people understand the power of their words, and how they can use words to tame their thoughts. I ask them to count silently from one to ten, and in the middle of the count, I ask them to say their name out loud, or to try naming state capitals. The point is, each time I take people through this exercise, they report that when they speak out loud, it interrupts the flow of their thoughts. That's how we should respond when negative thoughts attempt to overtake us. Instead of focusing on the negative and allowing your mind to go south, say out loud, "Stop! No more," or, "That's enough." It will short-circuit your thought process and remind you to focus on what is true and positive.

Many Christians allow their minds to be held captive by the words and thoughts of the devil, when they have the authority to shut his operation down. You must capture bad thoughts by speaking the Word of God. Tap into the creative ability God has given you, and speak His Word to counteract the enemy's attack.

You can be certain Satan will try to inject thoughts into your mind that are contrary to God's Word. Second Corinthians 10:5 says that we are to cast down imaginations and every high thing that exalts itself against the knowledge of God. In essence, that verse means it is our responsibility to get rid of every thought that is against God.

Also in that passage of Scripture, Paul advises us to bring "into captivity every thought to the obedience of Christ." It is clear, then, that negative thoughts should not be left unchecked, including memories of past mistakes and disappointments.

Remember, Satan is constantly trying to bombard you with negative thoughts. He is at war, trying to gain control of your mind and ultimately your life. If you don't open your mouth and defeat him with your words, you'll lose. When the doctor diagnosed me with cancer, it wasn't easy to win. I had to really work at it until I developed enough confidence and faith to produce results. If I had opened my mouth and agreed with the doctor, or spent more time telling people about my diagnosis, fear would have overtaken me. When you expect the worst, it has a way of showing up!

When you expect the worst, it has a way of showing up!

Let's look at a practical example of how words can change and rearrange circumstances. Suppose "Michael" is seeking a better job with better benefits, higher pay, and greater opportunity for advancement. Soon after his job search begins, he lands an interview with a prestigious Fortune 500 company. At first he's excited and eager to interview for the position. He's qualified and experienced—he knows he has a good shot at landing the job—but he has a problem with negative self-talk. While outwardly confident, he can't seem to stop telling himself, "You're not going to get the job. You're not good enough. What if they don't like you or the way you look?" Without realizing it, he is buying into Satan's plan for him to fail.

Michael mentions the interview to his friends. One of them says, "I heard that company doesn't pay very well." Michael ignores the comment and remains optimistic, but those words are still floating around in his mind. Instead of using the Scripture that says, "I can do all things through Christ which strengtheneth me" (Philippians 4:13), he allows the words of doubt, fear, and apprehension to control his mind, and his friends' comments don't help the situation. Another associate says, "I used to work there. I hated it." Still Michael says nothing. In the back of his mind, the negative thoughts continue to grow.

Finally, it's time for the interview. As a result of his focus on negative thoughts, Michael becomes nervous, leaving him less confident. Deep down inside, he thinks, *I'll never get this job*. He goes in and stumbles over his words, fidgets, and repeats himself. The interviewers are not impressed. Needless to say, he blows the interview and doesn't get the position.

Negative words created thoughts in Michael's mind that produced doubt. This affected his confidence, and ultimately caused him to experience the outcome he had imagined—failure. Being a better custodian of his thoughts, coupled with the power of God's Word, would have equipped him with the knowledge of how to respond. He could have literally talked himself into the job by building self-confidence.

I travel around the world preaching the Word of God, and I've come across many people who say, "I know the Bible says wealth and riches shall be in my house, but I just can't see myself in a mansion." This is how I respond: "Well, you don't have to worry about ever living in one. You've already talked yourself out of it!" You may think that's harsh, but it's reality. When a person wants to accomplish something but fails to plant Word-seeds in his mind and heart, he will likely never reach the intended goal. That's where confessions, or declarations, can help.

Right now, I want you to open your mouth and declare a few things. Use the authoritative power God has given you to make the following declaration:

Lord, I thank You for Your Word and I declare, right now, that it is the final authority in my life. I believe I can change my life through the power You have made available to me through Your Word. Lord, I ask You to reveal all truths to me as I seek You. I know that You are perfecting everything that concerns me, and I thank You, in advance, for the great life You have planned for me. It is more than I could ask, think, or imagine. From this day forward,

I will carefully choose the words I speak, hear, and see. I purpose in my heart to speak Your Word daily. Thank You for Your Word. I believe it will change my life and enable me to fulfill my purpose in life. I declare these things in Jesus' name. Amen.

If you're not accustomed to making declarations of faith, begin doing it until it becomes second nature. Look at the Scriptures you've written in your journal that apply to your specific circumstances. You may also want to add a few more to cover some of the general areas of your life. Some common areas include family, finances, favor, protection, wisdom, and so on. Write out your own declarations and make a commitment to repeat them daily until you see the changes you desire. You may not think what I'm suggesting is necessary, but if you're serious about living a victorious life, you'll get your journal right now and begin to turn to Scriptures you've recorded into confessions.

Next, devise a plan for when, where, and how often you will make confessions. I find that when I need an immediate breakthrough, making confessions several times a day is helpful.

Making confessions or declarations is an opportunity to change the course of your life. You will reach your divine destination if you embrace God's Word and allow it to change your thoughts, emotions, decisions, actions, habits, and character. You were born to fulfill God's purpose, and your journey begins with the Word of God.

> *You will reach your divine destination if you embrace*
> *God's Word and allow it to change your thoughts,*
> *emotions, decisions, actions, habits, and character.*

Think about the things that have been holding you back. Maybe there's something you want to accomplish, but you don't really believe it will happen. Think about the words that have been spoken to, and about you, over time. Consider the things you've been telling yourself lately. Maybe someone told you that you'd never amount to anything, and you believed them. Erase it! Start now. God can do more for the man or woman who believes than for the one who doesn't. The Bible says, "Everything is possible for him who believes" (Mark 9:23, NIV).

TAKE ACTION

When I played high school football, our team was tough to beat. We weren't the biggest or the fastest, but we had more confidence than any other team. We knew we could win. We said we would win, and we expected to win—every time. And in most cases, we did! The coach taught us an important lesson on using words to dictate our outcome. It's a poem called, "The Man Who Thinks He Can." These very words gave us the fuel we needed to be successful on the football field, and they can apply to anything in life you set out to do.

The Man Who Thinks He Can
by Walter D. Wintle

If you think you are beaten, you are.
If you think you dare not, you don't.
If you'd like to win, but think you can't,
It's almost a cinch that you won't.
If you think you'll lose, you're lost,
For out in the world we find
Success begins with a fellow's will;
It's all in the state of mind.
If you think you're outclassed, you are;
You've got to think high to rise.
You've got to be sure of yourself before
You can ever win a prize.
Life's battles don't always go
To the strongest or fastest man;
But sooner or later the man who wins,
Is the one who thinks he can.

If you want to experience the best life has to offer, make a quality decision to change your words. Don't be afraid of what others think or say. God will make sure you are not put to shame. He will always do exactly what He has promised, and whenever you take a stand to do God's will, you will receive a great reward.

If you speak and think positively, you will experience the quality of life you desire and the abundant life Jesus came to bring. Imagine the best, and the best will happen to you! It's time to put what you've learned into practice.

Review Nuggets

God wants you to live a life of abundance. He wants you to experience joy, peace, happiness, and love in your daily life. He wants you to have more than enough friends, family, love, and affection. He wants you to have more than enough wisdom, knowledge, righteousness, courage, and strength. He wants you to have more than enough food, clothing, transportation, recreation, and money. God is a *big* God. His plans for you are far better than you could ever imagine. However, without an understanding of what God desires, and how He operates, you won't receive everything He has set aside for you. Mastering your words and understanding their power to direct the course of your life is the key to mastering your mind. Taming your thoughts is only accomplished by speaking the Word of God. You must become a vigilant custodian of your thought life in order to keep Satan's words out of your mind.

Reading and meditating on God's Word is the only way to introduce God's thoughts into your life. Although positive thinking is beneficial, the highest level of thinking you can achieve is that which is governed and controlled by the Word. When you read and study the Bible, you're ingesting words that God has spoken specifically for you—words that have the power to change your destiny.

Foundation Scripture

For with God nothing is ever impossible and no word from God shall be without power or impossible of fulfillment.

Luke 1:37 (AMP)

Practical Application

This is a reality check to examine the impact your thoughts may be having on your life. I recommend that you move to a place where there are no distractions to focus carefully on your answers.

1. Are you entertaining thoughts that oppose God's Word?

2. Do you remember what led to some of the negative thoughts you've received?

3. How have negative thoughts impacted your life?

4. What are you willing to do to reverse the impact of negative thoughts?

5. If you could delete one thought, what would it be?

Step 2

Overhaul Your Thinking

Change Your Thinking— Change Your Life

When was the last time you really thought about your life and the direction in which you are heading? No matter where you are, whether you are experiencing success or failure, your mindset has a great deal to do with your position in life. The words you've heard over time have formed a thinking pattern that has set your course in a certain direction. If you aren't satisfied with where you are in life, it's time for you to develop a new way of thinking that lines up with God's Word. Unless your thinking changes, nothing in your life will change. With the multitude of negative messages available in today's society, you need every Word-based seed you can get!

YOUR MIND—THE CONTROL CENTER

Contrary to what religion may have taught you or what you may have heard growing up, it *is* the will of God for you to prosper in every way, from your health and finances to your relationships and career. Every area of your life should be an expression of abundant living. However, your life will only prosper to the degree that your soul prospers. Total-life prosperity won't happen if your mind doesn't prosper *first*.

It is the will of God for you to prosper in every way, from your health and finances to your relationships and career.

Your soul is the primary area the enemy attacks with words that are in opposition to God's Word. Your *soul* is where your mind, will, and emotions reside. So you can see why Satan's goal is to influence your thinking so your feelings are affected. Then your actions and decisions will move you in the wrong direction.

Your mind is the control center of your life, and in order to prosper and experience the good life, this critical area of your soul must line up with God's Word and reject the words and suggestions of the enemy. Some people may wonder how someone can be born again and still operate as he did before he accepted Jesus. Many times the problem lies within the soul.

Give careful consideration to this. The thoughts you act on have the potential to change your life's course.

GARBAGE IN, GARBAGE OUT

Your mind is the arena of faith where the battle of words is won or lost. It's the starting point for prosperity or poverty, healing or sickness, failure or success. It's up to you to reject the negative words the enemy tries to plant in your mind. If you find that your thoughts are producing failure rather than success, change the way you think.

Romans 12:1, 2 says:

I beseech you therefore, brethren, by the mercies of God, that ye present your bodies a living sacrifice, holy, acceptable unto God, which is your reasonable service. And be not conformed to this world: but be ye transformed by the renewing of your mind, that ye may prove what is that good, and acceptable, and perfect, will of God.

The apostle Paul used a strong word in that Scripture—*beseech*. That is a strong petition. The Amplified Bible says, "I appeal to you." In other words, Paul was saying, "I am begging you to accept this message and obey it." What he wanted us to understand is how we can be transformed by renewing our minds with new ideas and attitudes from God's Word. He recognized the importance of mind renewal to such a point that he literally begged this group of Believers to conform to God's way.

Renewing the mind is necessary to change your decisions and actions. If you are born again but don't invest the time and effort in renewing your mind, your actions will still mirror those of an unsaved man or woman.

Another reason to renew your mind is so you will know the will of God for your life. You can't discover His will when your mind is cluttered with ungodly thoughts and old thinking patterns. God needs a clear channel to communicate His plans and desires to you—a mind and heart that are aligned with His Word.

Changing the way you think isn't an overnight process. For most people, a negative mindset has been cultivated over many years. Don't become frustrated when you make a decision to change and find yourself facing new challenges. Be patient with yourself while going through this process. Continue feeding your mind and spirit with the Word of God, and you will start to form new thoughts and new patterns.

To prevent old ways of thinking from resurfacing, guard your mind. When negative thoughts enter your mind, cast them down with the Word of God. This requires consistency and discipline, but it's necessary to experience success.

Learn what God says about the mind of a born-again Christian. The Word says, "[you] have the mind of Christ" (1 Corinthians 2:16). Through understanding, you can walk in victory over negative thinking. As a Believer, you have the potential to operate in the same mental capacity and focus as Jesus! His mind was completely surrendered to, and governed by, the Holy Spirit. He didn't yield to sin or temptation, even though He was faced with them many times.

As an heir of salvation and a joint-heir with Christ, you don't *have* to succumb to negativity in your thought life. God has made tremendous power available to the born-again Christian who decides to change. The Holy Spirit will empower you to resist the thoughts of the enemy.

Doing something you've never done before requires change. It's futile to spin your wheels doing the same thing over and over and expecting totally different results. You must be proactive in changing your thoughts so you can experience the best God has for you. Make a quality decision to give your mind a complete overhaul.

CHANGE MUST TAKE PLACE

To reap the benefits of a renewed mind, there are five vital areas to consider. They are extremely important and will determine success or failure in many areas of your life.

1. Believe that God has a plan and destiny for your life.

God's plan for your life was established before the foundation of the world. Long before your parents ever met, God designed you for a purpose. Failure to believe this leaves an open door for Satan to convince you that your life is meaningless. If you fail to renew your mind, he may convince you to give up. You must know and believe that your life has a specific purpose. Ask yourself, *Am I on my way to my destiny?* Be cautious, and don't allow yourself to get stuck in a detour.

2. Believe that God's power within you is greater than any circumstance in your life.

It is easy to blame others for the condition of your life. Many people may agree with you, but that doesn't make it true. Rise up and take control of your thoughts and emotions. When negative things happen, speak the Word of God. I have experienced tragedy in my life, but I don't allow it to control me with bitterness, anger, and doubt. Troubles will come, but you can overcome all things through the Word of God. Handling life's circumstances in the wrong way will rob you of your peace and allow bitterness and resentment to replace it.

Troubles will come, but you can overcome all things through the Word of God.

I was hurt when my father went home to be with the Lord. The pain was almost unbearable. I knew I had to do something to keep from focusing on my grief, so I accepted an invitation to preach at a church in Tennessee. I left town for a few days to minister to others. As I ministered, I was nourished in the process. At night, when I returned to my room, grief tried to penetrate my thoughts. I knew if I allowed it to, it would paralyze me emotionally and spiritually. Instead, I fought by speaking the Word of God and staying focused on my calling to help others.

Allow the power of God inside you to change what's occurring around you. Don't allow the devil to control you through circumstances. Regardless of what may be going on in your life, if you'll nourish your spirit with God's Word, you can get through life's challenges and remain balanced in your emotions.

3. Believe that giving your best produces God's best for you.

I used to preach four sermons on Sundays, and travel all over the world to minister each week. There were times I would see double because I was so tired. But even in the midst of my fatigue, I wanted to give God my best, because I knew that He would give me *His* best in return. It wasn't long after we moved into our current facility, the World Dome, that God began flooding me with blessings. In fact, I asked, "Lord, what's going on?" He said, "I just wanted to let you know how much I appreciate your doing your best for Me. Now, I'm doing My best for you." John 10:27 says, "My sheep hear my voice, and I know them, and they follow me." This is how it works! Expect God's best by giving Him *your* best, and He will speak and guide your life.

4. Cultivate order and balance in your life by keeping your priorities in line with God's will.

More than half of all American marriages are failing because of wrong priorities. Matthew 6:33 says, "But seek ye first the kingdom of God, and his righteousness; and all these things shall be added unto you." Seeking first the Kingdom of God is His divine order. Your number one priority in life should be seeking His righteousness, and His way of doing things.

You can live a balanced life by keeping your priorities in line with God's will, which is His Word. There are six areas of priority:

- **Faith.** Build your relationship with the Lord through prayer, Bible study, and church attendance.

- **Fitness.** Obtain mental and physical health through regular exercise, proper rest, and diet.

- **Family.** Cultivate strong and happy relationships with your spouse, children, and other family members through daily communication and quality time together.

- **Fellowship.** Develop healthy relationships with friends who build you up and help you accomplish your goals in life. Do the same for them.

- **Finances.** Earn income in a career that brings you fulfillment and helps you accomplish your dreams. Of course, the best career is the one that God chooses for you.

- **Fun.** Get involved in recreational activities that bring you enjoyment. There is nothing wrong with enjoying good, wholesome fun.

5. *Believe that you are anointed to do all things.*

What does it mean to be anointed? It means that God has equipped you with burden-removing, yoke-destroying power. First Corinthians 2:12 says, "Now we have received, not the spirit of the world, but the spirit which is of God; that we might know the things that are freely given to us of God." If you are a Believer, you already have the mind of Jesus Christ and His anointing, which enables you to accomplish all things. In 1 John 2:20 it says, "Ye have an unction from the Holy One, and ye know all things." In other words, you have an ability from God to know all things. When your thinking is renewed, you are able to gain knowledge directly from Him, and when you renew your thinking, you will change your life!

Review Nuggets

There is a direct connection between the words you speak and your pattern of thinking. Your thoughts significantly impact your path in life. It is therefore important to renew your mind daily with God's Word. An increased relationship with Him will lead you to His divine plan for your life.

Renewing your mind is a process that you must purpose to do. If you desire to change your life, begin by changing the way you perceive yourself and others. Govern your thoughts by the Word of God, not by the negative words of others. As you progress, change will take place, and God's perfect will for your life will be revealed to you.

Foundation Scripture

But seek ye first the kingdom of God, and his righteousness; and all these things shall be added unto you.

Matthew 6:33

Practical Application

The battle of words is won or lost in the arena of your mind. It's up to you to reject the negative words the enemy plants in your mind: garbage in and garbage out. Review notes in your journal about the negative thoughts you are trying to eliminate. Have you made progress? Why or why not? Take this time to review, evaluate, and set your course. When those negative thoughts begin to invade your mind again, immediately replace them with the Scriptures you have written down. Paraphrase the Scriptures and begin confessing them more often. By doing so, you will prevent the negative thoughts from taking root. If a thought doesn't take root, it can't produce a harvest. The truths in God's Word will keep you in perfect peace and will ultimately produce a wonderful harvest.

Meditation Is Key to
Renewing Your Mind

Have you ever desired to change, but felt you couldn't? Do you believe certain behaviors are impossible to change? The truth is, nothing is impossible with Christ. You have at your disposal God's manual for life—His Word. It is the tool that will enable you to become completely whole and to accomplish your life's purpose.

Renewing your mind through meditation will lead you to success. Joshua 1:8 says that meditating on God's Word is the path to obtaining a prosperous life. However, meditation is an often-misunderstood concept. With so many perspectives on *what* meditation is, from New Age ideas to Eastern philosophies and religious practices, many are confused about this important aspect of their walk with God. Yet, meditation originated with God!

You're probably thinking, *So, Dr. Dollar, what does it mean to meditate?* Well, I'm glad you asked! As we've discussed, meditation is not just going quietly "within" to find a state of tranquility and peace. It's using the Word of God as a tool to find peace and solutions in your life. To *meditate* means to ponder, think about, and turn something over in your mind until you get understanding. It is not emptying your mind of all thoughts. On the contrary, when you meditate on the Word of God, you focus your thoughts on Scriptures and allow God to speak to you and give you revelation knowledge.

Meditating on God's Word is the way to reprogram your mind. Obtain a revelation of those Scriptures so they may be applied to your life. Focus your mind on the Word of God. This is the path to true and lasting change. It involves more than just casually reading over the Scriptures.

Through meditation, you gain wisdom and knowledge from God's Word that you would otherwise not have access to. The message behind each Scripture is illuminated and begins to penetrate your heart, giving you knowledge you would have never gained on your own.

New thought patterns don't form overnight. Renewing the mind requires consistency and a plan of action. *Practicing* meditation will give you the strength and knowledge to overcome negative thought patterns and live victoriously. Therefore, it's important for you to set aside time daily.

Renewing the mind requires consistency and a plan of action.

FORMS OF MEDITATION

There are several forms of meditation. First, there is the aspect of meditation called *pondering*. To *ponder* something is to think about it deliberately and carefully, to engage in contemplation. This happens when you take a Scripture and think about it over and over again. When you ponder a Scripture, you turn it over in your mind, "squeezing" out all the revelation knowledge contained in it. You can spend minutes, hours, days, and even longer, pondering a Scripture.

Meditation also includes asking the Lord to show you how certain Scriptures apply to specific situations in your life. It will take effort on your part to get the most out of your meditation time, but it is worth it. Start out with a few minutes a day, and then increase your time in meditation of Scriptures. You will be amazed at the level of understanding and revelation you receive as a result.

Another way to meditate on the Word is to pray aloud. There is a powerful connection between what you say, hear, and receive in your spirit. I call it the mouth-heart connection. The Word says that faith comes by hearing the Word of God (Romans 10:17). What better way to plant the Word in your heart and change your thinking than by speaking it? When you make faith confessions and pray the Word of God out loud, you hear it and receive it into your spirit. The more you do this, the more these words will begin to impact and change your thinking.

Taking time daily to make Word-based confessions from a tape, from a book of Scriptures, or directly from the Bible is critical to establishing your meditation regimen. Singing the Word through praise and worship songs is another way to meditate. When you speak or sing the Word, you are planting seeds that will help reverse negative thinking.

It might surprise you, but worry is a form of meditation. Worry means consistently pondering negative outcomes. Worry is the *opposite* of faith. Choosing to be concerned about circumstances instead of believing God's Word gives priority to worry in your life. However, you can overcome worry by familiarizing yourself with God's promises and meditating on them instead of on negative words or circumstances.

Can you imagine the things you could accomplish simply by changing your mindset and adjusting your perspective? By keeping the Word continually before your eyes, in your ears, and on your mouth, you can develop such a strong consciousness of doing things God's way that your whole mind becomes permeated with His thoughts. When this happens, your emotions and decisions will lead you to your divine destination.

CHANGE YOUR PERSPECTIVE, CHANGE YOUR LIFE

Renew is defined as "to make new or to restore to its original state." If the mind needs to be *renewed*, or restored to its original state, that means there was a time when it was not in need of renewal. In the beginning, Adam and Eve were clothed with the glory of God. They were blessed in every aspect of life—spirit, soul, and body. Their minds were whole and their hearts were pure, but once they sinned by disobeying God, they were no longer clothed in God's glory. Through Christ, redemption was

CHANGING YOUR WORLD
2500 BURDETT RD
COLLEGE PARK, GA 303

BATCH: 044
S-A-L-E-S D-R-A-F-T
73963691
907233000107

REF: 0998
CD TYPE: VISA
TR TYPE: PURCHASE
DATE: AUG 04, 09 13:09:39

TOTAL $11.20

ACCT: ************6612   EXP: **/**
AP: 00436A
NAME: JULIUS R GORDON JR

CARDMEMBER ACKNOWLEDGES RECEIPT OF GOODS
AND/OR SERVICES IN THE AMOUNT OF THE
TOTAL SHOWN HEREON AND AGREES TO PERFORM
THE OBLIGATIONS SET FORTH BY THE
CARDMEMBER'S AGREEMENT WITH THE ISSUER

THANKS FOR USING VISA

CUSTOMER COPY

made possible, and as a result, we have access to the wholeness God originally established for us.

When you renew your mind, you will enhance your understanding of life and how to operate in it. You are able to see things from God's perspective. This will change how you respond to situations and people. A person who has no knowledge of God's Word, and does not operate with a renewed mind, has no capacity for deeper levels of understanding. Therefore spiritual truths are impossible for them to comprehend.

God is love, and when you renew your mind, you will adopt a mindset of love. You will gain a fresh perspective on why God's way is the best path to choose. God's love working through you will enhance your perspective. You will gain a renewed ability to love others and exercise patience.

> *God is love, and when you renew your mind,*
> *you will adopt a mindset of love.*

Renewing your mind in the area of love will also give you a new understanding of who you are in Christ. When your mind has been transformed, you will rise above every natural, carnal circumstance and situation you may encounter. Renewing your mind will enable you to overcome negative circumstances and lead you to a brighter future.

Romans 12:2 tells us not to copy the behaviors and customs of the world, but to be new and different, with newness in all actions and thoughts. When you become a different person, you will have proof from your own experience of how beneficial and satisfying God's ways truly are.

To be a shining light in this world, you can't think or live like the world. Be a positive influence on others by demonstrating Christ-like character. Don't be easily moved by your circumstances. Instead, stand in faith and remain positive. Avoid conversations and activities that would hinder your progress. Refuse to hold on to old attitudes, and turn away from pride and fear altogether. As you renew your mind, you will build the faith to achieve more than you ever imagined.

Here are seven benefits to renewing your mind:

1. You see and understand things on a higher level.

According to Matthew 13:19, you are vulnerable to the enemy if you hear the Word and don't strive to receive understanding. A renewed mind enjoys great understanding.

2. You gain understanding of your rights as a child of God.

When you renew your mind according to the Word, you won't give any place to negative influences in your mind. As a result, you will access the blessings that God has promised you.

3. You refuse to accept defeat.

When you begin to renew your mind with the Scriptures, you will realize you are more than a conqueror through Jesus Christ, and you have authority over the enemy.

4. You refuse to walk in fear.

"For God hath not given us the spirit of fear; but of power, and of love, and of a sound mind" (2 Timothy 1:7).

5. You refuse to live in poverty.

God takes pleasure in the prosperity of His servants (Psalm 35:27). A born-again Christian should never be broke, because God doesn't want His children to suffer or be in lack. Renewing your mind to your covenant right to wealth is a key to your breakthrough in this area.

6. You refuse to put up with sickness.

Healing is your covenant right as a Believer. Meditating on Scriptures about God's promises on healing will give you the faith to overcome sickness and disease, and to walk in divine health.

7. You refuse burdens the enemy tries to put on you.

When you know that Jesus has removed all burdens, you will refuse to be weighed down by them. Renewing your mind and meditating on the Scriptures will give you access to victorious living. Dare to believe God's Word and experience change. Time and time again, God has proven that renewing your mind is the pathway to success. Embrace a new way of thinking that may be outside your comfort zone. Allow Him to prove His power in your life. You'll see. Your life will never be the same.

Renewing your mind is the pathway to success.

Review Nuggets

Meditation is the key to renewing your mind. When you meditate on the Word of God, you ponder (or think about) it, and turn it over in your mind, until you receive revelation about it. Allow the Word of God to become real in your heart through the practice of meditation. You will enjoy the results of positive change when you keep the Word of God before your eyes, in your ears and speak it out loud consistently. By changing your thinking, you will ultimately change your life and gain fresh understanding of God's Word, His ways, and His victory.

Foundation Scripture

This book of the law shall not depart out of thy mouth; but thou shalt meditate therein day and night, that thou mayest observe to do according to all that is written therein: for then thou shalt make thy way prosperous, and then thou shalt have good success.

Joshua 1:8

Practical Application

If you're not seeing the promises of God materialize in your life, it may be that your faith is not able to carry you through. However, through meditation, your faith will grow stronger and sustain you in every situation.

Look over your journal and the Scriptures you have been confessing. Ask God to give you more revelation concerning how the Scriptures relate to your life. Write down what He tells you, and act on the direction and wisdom He gives you.

Attain the Mind of God for Success

If you want to achieve your destiny, being born again isn't enough. You must learn how to develop and operate with the mind of Christ in order to create success in your life. The tools you need to do this were instilled in you before you were born.

Although your spirit is made new the moment you accept Jesus Christ into your heart, your mind must be renewed daily. The apostle Paul realized the importance of daily mind renewal; it contributed to his success. First Corinthians 15:31 says, "[I assure you] by the pride which I have in you in [your fellowship and union with] Christ Jesus our Lord, that I die daily [I face death every day and die to self]" (AMP). Paul made a decision to let go of his own will, thoughts, and emotions in exchange for something better. When you adopt God's thoughts, you adopt His ways, and your life will take a guaranteed path toward success.

It *is* possible to attain the mind of God. He is not some mysterious being that lives out in the universe somewhere. When Jesus comes into your life, His Holy Spirit takes residence inside your spirit. You literally become infused with supernatural potential! This includes having a supernatural mind, which is the mind of Christ (1 Corinthians 2:16).

You don't have to be governed by negative thinking for another day. Believe God, and receive the mind of Christ. Let His thoughts become your thoughts. Allow this to become reality in your life so you can begin living on a higher level, a level dominated by love, prosperity, and eternal life. When you allow God to give you the wisdom and insight you need daily, you position yourself to experience success and total fulfillment.

DEVELOP THE MIND OF CHRIST AS A STRATEGY FOR SUCCESS

I've made you aware of the importance of grafting God's thoughts into your mind. Through Christ you are made righteous. That means He has placed you in right standing with Him. The promises of God belong to you, and you have been empowered to prosper! Developing the mind of Christ is the path that will get you there.

The Word says that God is love (1 John 4:16). So the mind of God is always fixed on loving others. And Mark 12:30, 31 says:

> And thou shalt love the Lord thy God with all thy heart, and with all thy soul, and with all thy mind, and with all thy strength: this is the first commandment. And the second is like, namely this, Thou shalt love thy neighbour as thyself. There is none other commandment greater than these.

The basis for your every thought and action should always be the love of God. The abundant life that God predestined for you includes a multitude of blessings. Maintaining a mindset of love will allow God to operate in you and funnel His blessings through you to others. According to the Word of God, we are blessed to be a blessing to others. Love is the foundation that will take you to this level.

The basis for your every thought and action should always be the love of God.

In Philippians 4:8, God describes what the thoughts of the Believer should be:

> Finally, brethren, whatsoever things are true, whatsoever things are honest, whatsoever things are just, whatsoever things are

pure, whatsoever things are lovely, whatsoever things are of good report; if there be any virtue, and if there be any praise, think on these things.

The attributes of the mind of Christ are described in James 3:17 as "first pure, then peaceable, gentle, and easy to be intreated, full of mercy and good fruits, without partiality, and without hypocrisy." These attributes should be cultivated in every person's life. The love of God is the foundation. Let's take a closer look at these attributes:

1. The mind of God is pure.

God's mindset is one of purity; it is undefiled. You should strive to maintain a pure mind that is free from the polluting influences of the world. Guard your heart and mind against negative words. This includes the music you listen to, the movies and television programs you watch, and the people with whom you fellowship. Also, strive to develop purity in your thinking by entering into God's presence through prayer, praise, and meditation. When you consistently fellowship with Him, your mindset will begin to resemble His.

2. The mind of God is peaceable.

When you have a peaceable mind, you aren't consumed by conflict. The peaceable mindset seeks peace and avoids strife. Refuse to allow circumstances to dictate your level of peace. Instead, stand on God's Word and you will experience the peace of God in every situation. Exercising the love of God when people come against you, or offend you, will help you to maintain a peaceable mind. Also, refusing competitive jealousy and other aspects of strife with others will allow peace to dominate every area of your life.

3. The mind of God is gentle.

Jesus set such a good example for us by being gentle toward others. He operated with a sincere heart and in a spirit of love. A gentle person is considerate, tactful, gracious, kindhearted; one who is sensitive to the needs of others. God uses that kind of person to minister to others.

4. The mind of God is benevolent.

Jesus' objective was to serve others in love. He showed His lovingkindness and desire to help others through healing and deliverance, touching people in ways that changed lives. As you adopt this mindset, you may notice your desires changing so that you want to do things for others, even when it's inconvenient.

5. The mind of God is merciful.

When you show mercy toward others, it's easy for you to operate in love. Being merciful means being quick to forgive and to show compassion and tolerance toward others. It is important for you to develop this aspect of God's character to experience His blessings in your life.

6. The mind of God is fruitful.

Productivity should characterize the life of Christians and non-Christians alike. Jesus was extremely fruitful in His life and ministry. When your mind is fruitful, you gain ideas, concepts, and insights that propel you toward success. The Word of God *always* produces results. Consistently use the Word to renew your mind. You will become more productive on your job, more effective in your relationships, and able to fulfill the things God has called you to do.

7. The mind of God is steadfast.

So many people cave in and quit when things get hard, but a steadfast mind refuses to give up in the midst of challenging circumstances. Being steadfast means being unshakable, uncompromising, and unmovable from your stance of faith. Even when Jesus was faced with the brutal reality of dying on the cross, He remained steadfast and kept moving forward to accomplish His life's purpose.

8. The mind of God is honest.

Honesty really is the best policy. This isn't just a cliché; it's an established truth. You should strive to have a mindset that is honest and full of integrity, whether at work or at home. Be honest with others as well as yourself. Taking time to search your heart daily will keep you honest. Evaluate where you are in your renewal process. Check yourself and your relationships with God and others to be sure you're operating in truth. Being truthful is a requirement for building Godlike character.

Don't be surprised when you are attacked by negative thoughts from our enemy, Satan. This is bound to happen as you develop and strengthen a renewed mind. He would like nothing more than for you to respond to people and situations in ways that oppose Christ. For example, as you strive to maintain a pure thought life, don't be surprised if Satan tries to make ungodly suggestions to your mind. You may be tempted to look at something you know you shouldn't, or to listen to things that sow impure thoughts. In times like those, it is imperative to use the Word of God and *immediately* cast those thoughts down. You can't afford to let them linger.

Like Jesus, you can be fruitful and productive in the things you set out to do. As you go through this process, there may be times when you fail to respond appropriately. However, don't get discouraged. Instead, stay focused on the positive. God looks at your heart.

HOW WILL HAVING THE MINDSET OF GOD LEAD ME TO MY DESTINY?

Thinking like God will move you into a realm of success that you have yet to experience. A higher level of thinking creates a higher level of living. His thoughts will *always* propel you to new spiritual heights that guarantee a life of abundance.

When your mindset is in line with the Word, God can work on your behalf and speak to you clearly, telling you what to do in specific situations. Maybe you need wisdom to know if you should accept a job offer, or perhaps you feel God is speaking to you about relocating to another city or attending a certain church. These decisions are instrumental in fulfilling the will of God for your life.

*When your mindset is in line with the Word, God
can work on your behalf and speak to you clearly,
telling you what to do in specific situations.*

There are divine connections that God desires to bring to you. Sharpening your ability to hear Him clearly is critical for making the right decisions. When your thinking is in line with the Word, you create clear reception for God's voice. Your thoughts begin to mirror His thoughts. Soon, your desires become more like His. As He leads you, your discernment, or ability to make the right decisions, will become clearer.

IT'S TIME TO CHANGE

You may be born again and on your way to Heaven, but living in Hell on Earth. Your finances, family life, and health may be a mess. That isn't the way God wants you to live. His thoughts toward you are thoughts of peace and prosperity. Not much will change in your life when you trust doctors, the financial system of this world, and the words of popular magazines and television personalities more than you do the Word of God. Everything else has the potential to fail. However, God's Word will *never* fail! It *must* be the final authority in your life, and your thinking must be dominated by it. Only then will you fulfill God's plan for your life.

I challenge you to take an honest look at your life. Inventory your thoughts, motives, and desires, and ask yourself, "How does my thinking measure up to God's thinking?" If you're like me, you probably see areas you *know* are in need of improvement. Are you still responding the same old way when people do or say hurtful things? What about when you receive a negative report from a doctor or creditor? Asking questions like these will help you identify areas of weakness and show you where mind renewal is needed.

I want to give you some action steps to take that will help you maximize the mind renewal process. Here they are:

1. Become aware of what you think and believe.

Don't rely on someone else to tell you what your problem is. Examine the problems you have and execute a corrective course of action. Learning more about the way you think and how you respond to problems will give you an advantage and allow you to resolve issues in your life.

2. Make a conscious effort to become aware of how God wants you to think.

Research God's Word to find out what God expects from you in the area of your thinking. Maybe your responses have been inappropriate and you've made excuses for your behavior. Make a commitment to do whatever God tells you, and obey Him no matter how uncomfortable it may be.

3. Focus on godly thoughts throughout your day.

Develop an awareness of His presence. Focus on things that are good and of good report.

4. Remember the Word-thought connection.

Graft the Word into your heart and mind. It will give you the wisdom you need when you need it most.

5. Take action.

This is so very important. If you want change in life, you can't continue to live according to your old attitudes. Allow the Word of God to produce new thoughts, attitudes, and ideas in your everyday life. Just as exercise improves your health, a renewed mind improves your life.

Every time you make a conscious decision to respond God's way, your battles will get easier. It will take effort and practice on your part to set aside your old way of doing things and embrace the new. When you do, you will experience total fulfillment and success in life.

Review Nuggets

Establishing your thoughts on the foundation of God's Word is the starting point for change and success. This can be accomplished through meditation, prayer, and reading His Word.

With a renewed mind, you allow God's thoughts to dominate yours, thereby enabling Him to effectively lead you into His will for your life. It will set you on the path to your destiny!

Foundation Scripture

And be not conformed to this world: but be ye transformed by the renewing of your mind, that ye may prove what is that good, and acceptable, and perfect, will of God.

Romans 12:2

Practical Application

Adopting a new way of thinking can be quite a challenge, since we have spent most of our lives developing our old thinking patterns. Awareness is the key to change. Today, make an extra effort to become more aware of your thoughts. When you have a thought that opposes the Bible's teachings, pray to God about it. Ask for His wisdom and strength to help you eliminate ungodly thought patterns once and for all.

Become the Gatekeeper of Your Mind

There is power in positive thinking. Even the secular world has capitalized on this biblical truth. You can find a multitude of books on the power of a positive mindset in just about any bookstore. It amazes me to see the power of positive thinking operating in the lives of people who don't even know the Lord. They apply the principles of God's Word and get results. Why? Because the laws of the universe have been set in motion, and they work for *everybody*. If a Believer and an unbeliever drop an apple from the roof of a building, they will achieve the same results, because they are both subject to the universal law of gravity. Many of today's popular talk show hosts, authors, and motivational speakers have tapped into principles that many Christians have yet to grasp. By applying spiritual laws, they have accessed one of the most important truths of the Bible: the way a man thinks forms the outcome of his life. It's no secret that your thoughts shape your future.

FRAME YOUR FUTURE WITH POSITIVE THINKING

You may have grown up hearing a lot of negative words about yourself: words like, "You'll never amount to anything," "You'll never be able to do that," or "You just don't have what it takes." These words have the power to hinder or even paralyze your ability to succeed. If you give attention to these words long enough, you will begin to believe them. It is critical that once you identify negative talk about yourself, you shut it down immediately! Refuse to accept it. What God thinks about you is what matters most. And since He's a loving and forgiving Father and hates condemnation, you can be confident of His faith in you. Only by receiving *His* words are you able to frame your future for an abundant life.

> *Only by receiving* His *words are you able to frame your future for an abundant life.*

If your life seems to be moving in a more difficult direction than you desire, examine the things you listen to and think about most. Remember what happened in the Garden of Eden, when Adam hid himself from the Lord, and God asked him, "Where are you?" Adam responded by saying he was naked, so he hid himself. Then God asked him, "Who told you that you were naked?" You see, Adam entertained Satan's words and chose to believe him over God. The enemy's words influenced Adam's thinking. So now I ask you, Who has influenced your thinking? Who convinced you that God doesn't have a destination of prosperity for your life? Was it a parent, teacher, spouse, or coworker? Despite what they've told you, I encourage you to dwell on what God thinks. He made you, He knows you, and He has an amazing plan for your life.

Every success or failure you experience starts with your thoughts. Your mind is the control center for your success. If it is filled with the Word of God and a positive outlook, then you will experience a prosperous existence. *You* control your destiny.

BECOME A CUSTODIAN OF YOUR THOUGHT LIFE

Proverbs 4:23 admonishes us to guard our heart because out of it flow the issues of life. Issues are everything that is important. This Scripture also means you are to keep, or guard, your *soul*, the place where your mind, will, and emotions reside. You must do this for your own protection. Guarding your soul requires you to filter every thought through the Word of God, and it takes work.

The mistake many people make in the renewing of the mind is thinking that they can overcome negative thoughts with positive ones—that never works. Willpower alone won't keep negative thoughts from bombarding your mind. Neither will it keep you from thinking about things that aren't in line with the Word. The only way to get rid of ungodly thoughts is to use the Word of God to take hold of them and cast them down.

> *The only way to get rid of ungodly thoughts is to use the Word of God to take hold of them and cast them down.*

Knowing the Word is critical to being able to distinguish between the subtle suggestions of the enemy, your own thoughts, and what God says. Once you've identified a wrong thought, get to work. The apostle Paul described the formula for casting down thoughts. In 2 Corinthians 10:3–5 he wrote:

> For though we walk in the flesh, we do not war after the flesh: (For the weapons of our warfare are not carnal, but mighty through God to the pulling down of strong holds;) Casting down imaginations, and every high thing that exalteth itself against the knowledge of God, and bringing into captivity every thought to the obedience of Christ;

If not caught and evicted from your mind, negative thoughts will form *strongholds*, which are fortified houses of thoughts that have been nourished over a long period of time. When you don't deal with bad thoughts, they will eventually shape a pattern of thinking in your life that will lead you in the wrong direction. It won't be long before you begin to tell yourself, *I can't change; this is just how I am.* If you think this way, or you feel trapped in a cycle of addictive or destructive behavior, you can be sure that a stronghold exists somewhere in your mind and it must be torn down with the Word.

When thoughts that oppose the Word enter your mind, cast them down by speaking Scriptures out loud. Make bold declarations from the Bible, and serve the devil an eviction notice to release his influence on your thinking. You may have to do this several times a day, but consistency guarantees success. As you become more proficient at being a "gatekeeper" over your thought life, you will find the attacks easier to overcome.

There is a battle that takes place in the mind; the struggle is over word-seed. You will either listen to and accept the words Satan and the world suggest to you, or you will listen to and accept what God tells you in His Word.

Jesus wasn't exempt from Satan's temptation, but He is the ultimate example of a man who overcame in this area. In order to get complete dominion over His thought life, Jesus focused on God's will and destiny for His life. He utilized the Word of God skillfully to defeat Satan thoroughly. This is the same action that is required for you to gain victory over your thought life.

In Matthew 4:3, 4, you see that Jesus was tempted by Satan, yet He resisted him:

And when the tempter came to him, he said, If thou be the Son of God, command that these stones be made bread. But he answered and said, It is written, Man shall not live by bread alone, but by every word that proceedeth out of the mouth of God.

Think about this for a moment. Jesus had the power to do *exactly* what the enemy suggested. He very well could have turned the stones into bread, but instead of giving in to the suggestions of Satan, He spoke what was written in the Word.

The good news is, you walk in the same authority. Therefore, you are equipped to do the same thing as—and even greater things—than Jesus did! Find Scriptures that pertain to the area in which you are being attacked, and confess them whenever Satan tries to rise against you.

Through your faith and confidence in the Word, you will cause Satan to flee from you. He has no choice but to submit to the authority of the written Word of God.

CREATE YOUR ATMOSPHERE

If you aren't satisfied with the direction your life is taking right now, it's time to examine how you've been thinking. Find the areas in which you aren't experiencing success, and take some time to reflect on what you really think about your ability to progress. More than likely, if you are stagnated, you will find that your mindset is the cause.

How do you view yourself? Do you see yourself as more than a conqueror through Christ Jesus, or do you think you just don't have what it takes to be a success? Are you in a rut, paralyzed by negative thoughts? Who planted negative seeds in your thoughts? Maybe someone has told you you're not worthy of the promotion or the new house you desire, and you have accepted this. If so, it's time for you to create a new atmosphere for yourself, one permeated by the Word of God.

Remember, Satan will try to set a particular atmosphere in your life by trying to influence your behavior. He does this by speaking words in an attempt to affect your thinking. Once your mind is set in a particular direction, it won't be long before you will begin speaking those same thoughts about yourself and your situation.

There is a sequence to the way your destiny will unfold. It starts with words that produce your thoughts. Your thoughts produce your emotions, which produce your decisions and your actions. Your actions form your habits, which ultimately shape your character. Your character then leads you to your destination in life. It's vital for your life to be framed by the Word of God. Take steps to experience an overflow of the good life that God has designed for you!

Take steps to experience an overflow of the good
life that God has designed for you!

As I've said, words are spiritual containers that hold either fear or faith. Before you were born again, the words you spoke and allowed to influence your thinking came from the world's system of doubt, fear, and negativity. Then when you were born again you had to learn a new way of thinking and speaking by receiving new words based on God's Word. This new way of thinking will lead to a new way of living and produce the life you've always dreamed of. Create the life you want; live it in abundance, to the full, until it overflows.

Review Nuggets

There most assuredly is power in positive thinking. Just look at the number of books and magazines that address the benefits of a positive mindset. Even a number of reality television shows capitalize on this.

Your mind is the control center of your life. Your success or failure originates with your thinking. For this reason, it is critical that your thinking be influenced by the Word of God instead of by the world's system, which is filled with fear, doubt, and unbelief. While you can't stop negative thoughts from coming to your mind, you can control whether they have a long-term place in your thought life. By becoming the gatekeeper of your mind, you can filter out ungodly thoughts and suggestions. When negative thoughts come, cast them down by speaking the Word of God.

Foundation Scripture

Beloved, I wish above all things that thou mayest prosper and be in health, even as thy soul prospereth.

3 John 1:2

Practical Application

A prosperous life starts with a prosperous mind. Take ten minutes every day this week to examine your thinking; your thinking determines your future. Ask the Holy Spirit to show you the issues, such as relationships, losing weight, or meeting a financial goal, that may be holding up your progress in a particular area. Begin to renew your mind by resetting your thinking according to the Word. Write down what God reveals to you about your thinking, and use your journal to chart the changes.

How Thoughts
Shape Your Life

Every day, the world's images and words bombard your mind. If you turn on your television or radio or pick up a newspaper or magazine, you will find that the enemy is constantly trying to influence you. We've established that he does this by planting the wrong seeds in your mind. Even driving down the street, you are confronted with billboard advertisements that can influence your thinking. All these things will begin to shape your thoughts. You can prevent those thought-shaping images from becoming imbedded in your mind by casting them out.

I want you to understand something now so you can experience the best God has for you: Jesus said He came so He could provide you with His best! God wants you to have an abundance of the anointing in every area of your life—in health, family, job, and finances—to the full, until it overflows. This is the path that will lead you to your destination.

Words are seeds that are planted in your heart. That's why the Bible says to keep, or *guard*, your heart with *all diligence*, because out of it are the issues of life (Proverbs 4:23). Think about it . . . If you are like most people, you probably grew up being exposed to a multitude of images that were far from the Word. Most likely, your parents and family didn't know anything about those things and may have even unknowingly encouraged you to indulge in negative thinking. When I was growing up, there were no real controls placed on the things I received into my mind. I wasn't aware of the impact that words and other influences had on my thinking and actions.

Growing up without clear-cut boundaries or knowledge of how thoughts shape your attitude and ultimately your future can prove to be very dangerous. In fact, it can produce a generation of people prone to ungodliness and failure. This is not God's will. He has given us His Word as the instruction manual to help us renew our minds so we can experience success in every area of life. It is up to us to input the information so we can receive the benefits.

THE BATTLE THAT RAGES WITHIN

There is a battle going on right now for control over your mind. Your enemy—Satan—is after your thoughts. His ultimate goal is to plant seeds of doubt, fear, unbelief, and sin in your mind so that he can exert *his* will in your life. He does this by making suggestions—things that may feel or look good to you, but are really a trap to set you up for disaster. Satan is not a creator, but he knows that his words have power. He uses music to get his words into the thoughts of people. He also uses television, which should be used to "tell-a-vision" when used for God's purposes. However, Satan has corrupted it to tell his own vision. He knows that if he can just get you to think about the wrong things, he's got your attention. Once your mind is programmed according to his system, he can get you moving in the wrong direction and away from the will of God for your life.

There is a battle going on right now for control over your mind.

On the flip side, God wants you to get *His* thoughts planted in your mind. That's done by getting *His* Word, keeping it in front of your eyes, in your ears, and coming out of your mouth. Programming your mind with the Word will set you on the path that leads to the good life.

The ultimate battle is for the Kingdom of God that is within you. Your heart is the ground that produces life or death, and words are the seeds that will grow and become the harvest. By keeping your mind guarded against the words of Satan, you will protect your heart and reap the harvest you want.

THE POWER OF SUGGESTION

Satan's assault against our minds is nothing new. His most powerful weapon is suggestion. He is *very* subtle, and uses things that often seem harmless in order to bring your thinking under his influence.

Adam and Eve are the first biblical examples of people who allowed the enemy to influence their thinking away from the will of God for their lives. Their decision to ignore God's instruction and instead receive the lies of the devil was responsible for their fall. Genesis 3:1–7 gives the account:

> Now the serpent was more crafty than any of the wild animals the LORD God had made. He said to the woman, "Did God really say, 'You must not eat from any tree in the garden'?" The woman said to the serpent, "We may eat fruit from the trees in the garden, but God did say, 'You must not eat fruit from the tree that is in the middle of the garden, and you must not touch it, or you will die.'" "You will not surely die," the serpent said to the woman. "For God knows that when you eat of it your eyes will be opened, and you will be like God, knowing good and evil." When the woman saw that the fruit of the tree was good for food and pleasing to the eye, and also desirable for gaining wisdom, she took some and ate it. She also gave some to her husband, who was with her, and he ate it. Then the eyes of both of them were opened, and they realized they were naked. (NIV)

I want you to look carefully at this Scripture so you can see the progression of Adam and Eve's fall. First, notice that Satan is crafty. His approach is not always obvious. That is why it is so important to be grounded in the Word well enough to be able to discern his suggestions. This is critical because your thinking is the absolute cornerstone of your life.

Remember that Satan's thought injections may sound good, but they always oppose God's Word. Notice that his first question to Eve was, *"Did God really say . . . ?"* He injected a thought that contradicted the exact instructions God had given her and Adam—do not eat from the Tree of the Knowledge of Good and Evil (the tree in the middle of the Garden). His suggestion was designed to make her question God. Eve's first response was to speak God's Word back to Satan (she was on the right track here), but she gave in after Satan replied that she would not surely die, even though God's *Word* said otherwise.

After Eve received the word-seed the devil planted in her mind, a desire was created that played on her emotions. The Word says that when she *saw* that the fruit looked good, she gave in to her feelings and ate it. Then she gave some to her husband to eat as well. Once their disobedience was complete, their eyes were opened and they realized they were naked. The glory of God that had blanketed them left, and the curse entered the Earth. Satan's mission was successful.

Satan's strategy is no different today than it was thousands of years ago in the Garden of Eden. He will try to get the same thing to happen in your life. He makes suggestions that oppose the Word of God and gets you to give attention to them. Once the thought-seed takes root in your mind, your emotions are affected, and eventually you take action that leads you out of God's will for your life, like Adam and Eve did. God's original plan for their lives wasn't death. It included eternal life and total dominion over the Earth. Their openness to negative thoughts caused them to get on the wrong path. You don't have to make the same mistake. Cast down Satan's suggestions and replace them with the Word of God.

> *Cast down Satan's suggestions and replace*
> *them with the Word of God.*

USE YOUR IMAGINATION!

God has given you an imagination so you can see yourself walking in all that He has promised you in His Word, so start building your future with Scriptures. Consider this: if you think, *I'll never get out of this situation*, then you never will. If you have "failure thinking," you're going to fail. However, if you think in terms of success, you will be successful. You are a free moral agent; you have the choice and you're making it! If what you're doing is not working, now is the time to change the way you think.

In Genesis 11, God confused the language of the people because they had purposed in their minds to build a tower to heaven (v. 4–6):

> And they said, Go to, let us build us a city and a tower, whose top may reach unto heaven; and let us make us a name, lest we be scattered abroad upon the face of the whole earth. And the LORD came down to see the city and the tower, which the children of men builded. And the LORD said, Behold, the people is one, and they have all one language; and this they begin to do: and now nothing will be restrained from them, which they have imagined to do.

They demonstrated the power of the imagination to literally create reality. They fixed their minds on an idea, and their actions followed suit.

Have you ever thought about what would happen if you set your mind on God's Word, allowed it to shape your mindset, and then set out to become what you imagined? If you did, you would become the man or woman God created you to be! God's Word is the final authority in a Believer's life, and it has the power to change you from the inside out. Change your mind and you will change your life.

God's Word is the final authority in a Believer's life, and it has the power to change you from the inside out.

While using your imagination is critical to establishing a prosperous future for yourself, it is also important to cast down imaginations that try to override godly images in your mind.

Don't sit around picturing yourself doing something outside the will of God. It could be a certain activity that you found pleasurable in your past, or it could be something you want to say to someone who has hurt you. The moment a thought that opposes God's Word tries to enter your mind, refuse it by speaking the Word of God. Speaking Scriptures releases the power of God against unwanted thoughts. This is what allows you to tear down strongholds and wrong imaginations. You have authority over your mind. You are *not* at the mercy of Satan and his words.

Exercising your authority is an act of your will. You must make a decision beforehand to be ready to challenge negative thoughts with the Word. By doing this, you put the enemy on notice that *you're* in control, not him, and that you won't be led astray.

Review Nuggets

Guarding your heart and setting boundaries for what you allow to enter into your thoughts will put you on the path to your destiny. Changing your old way of thinking requires action on your part. Something as simple as taking steps to monitor what you watch on television, or even the type of music that you listen to, will help you succeed! Apply the Word of God to any area of your life that is in need of renewal. *Immediately* replace any negative thoughts and wrong imaginations with the Word of God. Recite God's Word daily. He has wonderful things in store for you, once you are positioned on the road to your destiny.

Foundation Scripture

Casting down imaginations, and every high thing that exalteth itself against the knowledge of God, and bringing into captivity every thought to the obedience of Christ.

2 Corinthians 10:5

Practical Application

Do you struggle to control ungodly thoughts? Consider what you watch on television or listen to on the radio. Do you read books or articles that oppose godly thinking? Write a list of the ungodly messages you have accepted over time. Make a specific plan to eliminate these influences. Put your plans into action for twenty-one days, and each day write a brief summary of your progress. You'll be encouraged by the results!

Step 3

Take Charge of Your Emotions

Understand
Your Emotions

Everyone has moments in life when emotions get out of control. It is not surprising to encounter circumstances in life that cause us to become frustrated, sad, or even angry. At the same time, I'm sure you've experienced many positive things that caused your emotions to soar. The key is to refuse to allow your life and decisions to be governed by your emotions—good or bad. God doesn't want His children living emotionally led lives. He wants us to have control over our emotions and submit them to His Word.

Contrary to what you may have been taught, emotions are not bad. Emotions are feelings caused by either pain or pleasure. They are designed to move you in a certain direction. They move you to make decisions that will either positively or negatively affect your future. Emotions move you either toward or away from the will of God for your life.

Often, particularly in religious circles, there are two extremes where emotions are concerned. Christians either allow their lives and their relationship with God to be ruled by their emotions, or they mistakenly believe that any show of emotions is sinful. Neither of these is a correct understanding.

Your soul is comprised of three compartments: mind, will, and emotions. God created you with the capacity to experience emotions. Problems arise when your decisions are based on those emotions. That's why getting your emotions in line with God's Word is so important.

Emotions are neither good nor bad. I like to use fire as a concept to illustrate this point. Fire itself is not good or bad; it simply depends on how and where it is used. When used in a positive way, fire can provide warmth and comfort. When placed in the wrong hands or allowed to burn unsupervised, it can cause destruction. It's the same way with emotions. When kept in proper context, feelings can draw you closer to God and your destiny. However, when you allow your emotions to control you, you will continually make decisions that are detrimental to your future.

When kept in proper context, feelings can draw you closer to God and your destiny.

THE WORD-THOUGHT-FEELING CONNECTION

The way you think determines the course of your life, and your thinking is framed by the words you hear and speak. Proverbs 23:7 says, "For as he thinketh in his heart, so is he." If you consider why you think the way you do and take time to carefully examine your words, I think you will see a clear connection between the words you say and hear and what you believe. For example, if you listen to worldly music all the time, your thinking will be influenced by those secular lyrics. If you associate with people who speak words of doubt and unbelief, don't be surprised if you find it difficult to believe God's Word in the face of challenging situations. The words you hear and speak are seeds that will produce a good or bad harvest in your life.

Negative words produce negative thinking. Negative thinking produces negative feelings and emotions, which produce negative decisions. Negative decisions produce negative actions, which produce negative habits. Negative habits produce negative character, which leads you to a negative destination. This is why it is so important to guard your heart from ungodly people and other dangerous influences.

For example, let's say a man purchases a new car, and while traveling down a busy street, another driver crashes into him and severely damages his car. He gets so angry about it that he gets out of his car and punches the reckless driver. Long story short, the reckless driver presses charges against the man, and the man is arrested. He loses his job, and because he often allows his emotions to get the best of him, his wife leaves him. His emotions moved him in a direction that was opposite of God's will for him and resulted in serious, and unnecessary, consequences.

You have probably experienced countless situations in which you allowed your emotions to drive your decisions with unfavorable, and sometimes disastrous, results. Maybe it was in the area of impulsive spending, overeating, or saying something in a moment of anger and causing someone pain. When emotions spin out of control, they can cause tremendous damage to others and ourselves.

JESUS CAN RELATE

The good news about emotions is that Jesus can relate to many of the emotional challenges we face. Sometimes people forget that, although Jesus was God in the flesh, He was also a human being who possessed a mind, will, and *emotions*!

Hebrews 4:15 says, "For we have not an high priest which cannot be touched with the feeling of our infirmities; but was in all points tempted like as we are, yet without sin." Jesus experienced most of the emotions that you and I go through. He was tempted to give up, cave in, and quit. He experienced depression, anxiety, fear, and other emotional challenges (Mark 14:32–35, AMP). However, He didn't yield to the negative emotions He felt. Instead, He overcame them.

Temptation is pressure applied to your flesh that impacts your thinking and moves you away from God's will. It is Satan's way of pressuring you to change your mind about believing what God has said. Many married men get into trouble in this area because they don't realize that the cute little secretary that walks past their desks is simply a temptation. Often, instead of turning away from the seduction and casting wrong thoughts down with God's Word, men yield to the temptation and end up in a compromising situation with someone other than their spouse. When you accept Satan's suggestions into your mind, your emotions will be affected, and you will eventually make bad decisions.

BE READY FOR THE ATTACK

Christians are the prime target for Satan's fiery darts because he wants them to abandon their promised destiny. Satan strikes the soul, where a person's mind, will, and emotions reside. His primary goal is to confuse a person's thinking so that person will put more confidence in feelings than in God's Word. Depression, fear, and worry are all tools Satan uses to weigh us down.

Depression is actually the result of external pressure that finds its way into your heart. I remember a time in my life when I had a serious battle with this negative emotion. At the time, I was a therapist, and I dealt with mental health patients on a regular basis. After listening to my patients' sad stories, I often found myself trying to alleviate the stress with food. Apple pies were my "escape," and the sugar high that I experienced from eating them provided relief for me. However, after several months and added inches to my waistline, I had to admit this was not the correct way to deal with the stresses I experienced as a counselor. Eating my way out of it was not the answer!

If you struggle with negative emotions such as depression and fear, take heart, because you are not alone. One of the greatest emotional attacks Jesus ever experienced was when He was in the Garden of Gethsemane prior to His crucifixion. Mark 14:32–35 describes what happened during the most stressful time of His life:

> Then they went to a place called Gethsemane, and He said to His disciples, Sit down here while I pray. And He took with Him Peter and James and John, and began to be struck with terror and amazement and deeply troubled and depressed. And He said to them, My soul is exceedingly sad (overwhelmed with grief)

so that it almost kills Me! Remain here and keep awake and be watching. And going a little farther, He fell on the ground and kept praying that if it were possible the [fatal] hour might pass from Him. (AMP)

If depression is active in your life, turn your eyes to Jesus and consider what He went through. The Scripture says His sweat was "as it were great drops of blood" because of the tremendous pressure He endured (Luke 22:44). Jesus was terrified, depressed, and overwhelmed with grief. However, He responded to the pressure by praying. The Bible says He continued pressing forward toward the will of His Father. Jesus refused to let His emotions stop Him from fulfilling the will of God for His life.

Satan tried to get Jesus to walk away from God's divine plan for Him, and he wants to do the same thing to you. When you allow your life to be governed by your emotions, you put yourself in a dangerous position. Satan will not hesitate to attack your emotions, particularly when you are at a vulnerable point in your life, but like Jesus, you have what it takes to resist and overcome.

WHEN THE PRESSURE IS ON

When your emotions try to lead you in the wrong direction, you must resist with the Word of God. Examine the words and thoughts that may have opened the door to the emotional attack. Even when you are feeling weary or discouraged, you must keep going forward. You can't afford to get sidetracked by negative emotions. You have to say, *I'm going to accomplish what God called me to do, no matter what!*

You can't afford to get sidetracked by negative emotions. You have to say, I'm going to accomplish what God called me to do, no matter what!

Jesus kept going forward and He kept on praying, and He will empower you to do the same during life's trying situations. It may hurt at times, and you may be crying as you go, but the key is to keep moving. Don't allow yourself to be paralyzed by an emotional attack.

God has set you free from the curse of the law. You have been set free from every bondage. Read what God's Word declares about you as a Believer, and start saying it. Confess out loud that Jesus is the Lord of your life and that you are no longer subject to these things.

Isn't it good to know that you don't have to be ruled by your emotions? God loves you and is personally interested in every aspect of your life, including your emotional well-being. The abundant life He has prepared for you includes wholeness and freedom, so when you are feeling down, don't run away from God—run to Him.

> *God loves you and is personally interested in every aspect of your life, including your emotional well-being.*

Negative feelings come from thinking the wrong thoughts after receiving the wrong words into your spirit. In order to get rid of *any* negative emotion, whether it is depression, fear, anxiety, or anger, it is absolutely critical that you change your mindset. Romans 12:2 states we are transformed by the renewing of our minds. The Word of God is the mind renewal system God wants you to use in order to reprogram your thought process and access healthy emotions.

Don't hang around people and influences that saturate your mind with bad reports. You can't afford to fellowship with people who constantly speak doubt and unbelief. If you do, those influences will begin to affect you. If you are in the midst of an emotional attack, the last thing you need to do is talk about your concerns with people who don't know the Word of God. They will only fuel the fire and compound the problem. Instead, allow God to govern your thinking.

When the pressure comes, resist it by speaking Scriptures that correspond with the issue you are dealing with. For example, if you are feeling depressed and burdened, meditate on Isaiah 60:1 which says, "Arise [from the depression and prostration in which circumstances

have kept you—rise to a new life]! Shine (be radiant with the glory of
the Lord), for your light has come, and the glory of the Lord has risen
upon you" (AMP)! You can't continue to walk around depressed when
you meditate and confess that Scripture!

The Word of God is powerful, and when you plant it in your heart
and speak it in faith, it will eradicate every negative emotion.

Review Nuggets

God gave you emotions, but He never intended for your life to be governed by them. As a Believer, God has given you authority over your emotions. While the enemy will attack your soul, you don't have to yield to his attempts to influence how you feel. Speak the Word of God when your emotions are under attack. Keep your feelings submitted to God's Word, and you can avoid making emotional decisions that will lead you out of God's will for your life.

Foundation Scripture

For as he thinketh in his heart, so is he.

Proverbs 23:7

Practical Application

Your thoughts will determine your feelings. Write down the emotions you've experienced today, whether positive or negative. Reflect on the events that affected your emotions. Ask God to guide you through the thoughts that produce your feelings. Pray, ask for forgiveness, and repent of any negative feelings you may have experienced—especially those of bitterness, unforgiveness, and anger toward others. As you continue to apply the Word of God to your circumstances, write in your journal the changes you are beginning to see in yourself.

Deal With Negative Emotions

The root of negative emotions is actually a sense of powerlessness. No matter what negative emotions you may deal with in your life, the root of it must be eliminated for you to experience freedom in this area.

There are three main areas in which the devil will try to convince you that you are powerless. First, he wants you to believe that you can't change your circumstances. He may try to convince you that your life is as good as it gets. Second, he wants you to think you cannot change different aspects of your personality. When you tell yourself, "I can't change; this is just how I am," you lock yourself into a prison of negative feelings and hopelessness. Third, he will try to convince you that you can't do anything to change your areas of weakness.

All three of these suggestions are lies! You are *not* powerless, you *can* have a better life, and you *will* become stronger. You don't have to fall for Satan's deceptive tactics ever again. God has given every Believer the tools necessary to overcome negative emotions. There is nothing that cannot be made better through faith and the Word of God; but it is up to you to use the authority God gave you.

God has given every Believer the tools necessary to overcome negative emotions.

Just as you have authority over your circumstances—your finances, physical body, or relationships (at home and at work)—you also have authority over your emotions. Debt, lack, poverty, sickness, and disease have to bow to God's authority, as do emotions. Jesus died so you could have a better, more rewarding life. That includes living a life unhindered by negative emotions.

Authority is the God-given right to command or rule. In the beginning, God gave man authority. When Adam turned his authority over to Satan in the Garden of Eden, he forfeited his God-given dominion and opened the door to the curse, which includes being emotionally driven. Jesus came to reverse the damage done by Adam's act of treason, and restore the authority that was lost in the Garden. You have been set free from the curse of the law, which includes negative emotions and depression. The baton of authority has been passed to you. Use it!

Emotions that are not governed by the Word of God can become a major enemy to God's plan for your life. When you allow your emotions to take charge, they will direct you away from God's wonderful destiny for you. If you find you aren't experiencing God's blessings, you need to examine your emotions and see where they are leading you. It could be you are taking a detour from the path God has etched out for you.

The Bible says the enemy comes to steal, kill, and destroy (John 10:10). He wants to discourage you and instill in you an attitude of failure. When stress is internalized, it leads to depression, and that hurt is the tool Satan uses to rob you of what God has for you. Any time you experience hurt for long periods of time, know that you are being robbed of what God has planned for you. Making decisions while you're hurting can sometimes lead you away from God and further into disappointment.

The potential for you to experience hurt will always be there. However, when you handle the situation properly, it won't be able to affect you by penetrating your spirit. In order to be continually victorious in life, you must develop the ability to quickly dismiss things people do that hurt you. What matters is how you respond to challenges when they arise. By making the Word the final authority and respond-ing in the love of God, you will be successful in overcoming hurt.

In order to be continually victorious in life, you must develop the ability to quickly dismiss things people do that hurt you.

BECOME EMOTIONALLY INVINCIBLE

If you have been hurt, the good news is you don't have to remain trapped in the prison of hurt feelings. You can be emotionally invin-cible because Jesus made a way out! Use the Word of God to effectively take authority over negative feelings. Align your heart and mind to agree with Him, and things will begin to change.

You can be emotionally invincible because Jesus made a way out!

The Word is the gateway to success and abundant life. Give particular attention to whom you spend time with. It may be you should stop hang-ing around certain people. You have to decide how you will change your thinking and respond to life. Consider the things that influence your life and decisions, and make adjustments where needed.

Contrary to popular beliefs, you can control your thought life. You aren't subject to bad thoughts. Though they may come, you don't have to let them reside in your mind. It is up to you to use the Word skillfully to cast down ungodly thoughts.

For example, you may have been hurt by someone you were in a relationship with, and the feelings of rejection are still weighing you down. The devil may be telling you you're no good, or that you'll never experience the joy of having a great relationship. Don't allow yourself to give in to those feelings! Stay above them. You can do this by *immediately* speaking Scriptures that counteract those thoughts when they come.

Get a concordance and search the Bible for Scriptures pertaining to God's undying love for you. He will never leave or forsake you. Don't allow wrong thoughts to linger in your mind. Keep speaking the Scriptures, and take those negative thoughts captive. As you begin to replace negative thoughts with God's thoughts, the feeling of rejection will diminish and eventually go away. As you continue to renew your mind, your emotions will follow, and you will experience victory over the enemy's emotional attacks.

The first step to becoming emotionally invincible is to be honest about what you are feeling. You have to identify where you are before you can go further. Don't deny your emotions—they are real. Instead, acknowledge your feelings. Don't give place to the enemy in your life by entertaining fear or insecurity. Keep your mind stayed on God and His Word.

When my dad died, it was a perfect opportunity for my emotions to go crazy. I did give in for a moment, but I had to get up and keep going. I kept every speaking and preaching engagement because there were people who needed to hear the Word. It was hard, but like Jesus, I prayed and kept going forward. I had to make up my mind that I would get through it and be strengthened by God's love and His Word. I knew Dad was okay and I would see him again. Continuing to fulfill God's will was my priority. I made a conscious decision not to allow my emotions to dictate my thoughts and actions.

If you are ever going to move forward in life, you'll have to deal with things that have hurt you. You can't sweep them under the rug. This may mean forgiving someone who did you wrong years ago, or letting go of something someone said to you as recently as this morning. The important thing to remember is that if you *don't* deal with those things that have hurt you, you won't reach your final destiny. You can't control everything that happens in life, but you *can* decide whether you will receive it and how you will respond. If you speak and meditate on the Word, your thoughts and emotions will line up with it. Then you will be on the right course to fulfilling your purpose.

If you don't deal with those things that have hurt you, you won't reach your final destiny.

RESOLVE THE ANGER CONFLICT

Anger is another emotion Satan uses to move people away from the will of God for their life. We've all experienced it, and likely acted out on it in the wrong way at one time or another. Anger itself is not necessarily bad, but how it's directed can be the issue.

There are people in prison right now because their anger prompted them to commit a crime. Yet while anger can be directed in a negative way, the Bible makes reference to anger in ways that aren't necessarily negative. Ephesians 4:31, Psalm 37:8, and Psalm 4:4 instruct us to handle and direct anger properly. Ephesians 4:26 says, "Be ye angry, and sin not: let not the sun go down on your wrath."

Jesus got angry when He entered the temple and the moneychangers were buying and selling goods in God's house (Mark 11:15-17). However, when you examine Jesus' response, it becomes clear that His anger was justified; it moved Him to take righteous action and set God's house in order. God knows you will get angry at one time or another, but how you handle it will make all the difference.

Remember, fire can be either positive or negative. It can heat a home or burn it down. Anger is the same way; it can move a person to take righteous actions, as Jesus did; or it can push someone toward unrighteousness.

Any time anger moves you out of the love of God and into selfishness, manipulation, or violence, it's *wrong*. Yet anger can move you in a positive direction. For example, debt, lack, sickness, poverty, and any other form of oppression should anger you.

To sit back and allow Satan to harass you, your loved ones, or other members of the Body of Christ could actually be considered sin. Jesus never put up with the devil. He continually drove him out of His presence. You should do the same. When you develop a mindset that refuses to put up with the devil's attacks, you will experience righteous anger. It should always move you to take action based on the Word of God. By taking authority over the enemy and casting him out of your finances, body, family, and life, you are using your emotions in the appropriate way.

Righteous anger should always move you to take
action based on the Word of God.

Some people don't experience victory in their lives because they tolerate Satan and his attacks. In Old Testament times, Nehemiah got angry about what the Israelites were going through, and it motivated him to do something about it (Nehemiah 5:6–9). It is appropriate for you to be angry at any circumstance that does not line up with God's Word. Here are three keys to help you understand, and effectively deal with anger:

- Control your feelings, and never act solely on the basis of emotions. Carefully consider the appropriate response.
- Don't act in haste, and don't allow anger to fester.
- Realize that you are much more vulnerable to sin when you are angry.

By distinguishing between appropriate and inappropriate anger, you can better use this emotion. Keep these keys at the forefront of your thinking to ensure that your actions spring out of the right motives. Anger doesn't have to control you. Instead, you can have dominion over it, just as Jesus did.

STUCK IN A RUT AND SINGIN' THE BLUES

Another emotion Satan uses to keep people paralyzed in life is depression. This destructive emotion has no place in the lives of God's children. Depression is a result of external pressures and comes from meditating on things that weigh you down.

If you want to change how you feel, you've got to change how you think. Unlike those who don't know Jesus, Christians have the weapon of God's Word to combat depression. When you know what God has said in His Word, you have something to hold on to in the midst of trouble. As a believer, you don't have to accept depression.

Proverbs 4:20–23 instructs you to pay close attention to God's Word and guard your heart. That means you need to be very careful about what you see, hear, and speak. Don't repeat bad reports or accept words that make you feel bad. Don't dwell on a particular situation by rehearsing it to yourself. Negative self-talk is a sure-fire way to stay depressed. Instead, make confessions from God's Word on a consistent basis. Speak to your problems rather than about them. Mark 11:23 says to ask for what you want by faith, believe you will receive it, and you will have it. In John 16:24, Jesus says when you believe that you receive in your heart what you have asked from God, joy will be released in your life that will dispel depression.

Speak to your problems rather than about them.

Sound an alarm to the enemy today that you refuse to give in to your emotions. Every time Satan pressures you to give in to selfishness, depression, or inappropriate anger, open your mouth and speak God's Word. You don't have to stay stuck in a rut another day. God loves you, and He has made provisions for you to be free from negative emotions forever. Use your authority and start trampling the devil. You don't have to ever be hurt again!

Review Nuggets

When you feel powerless, you are more likely to give in to negative emotions. Don't yield to hurt, anger, and depression. Instead, fill yourself with God's Word and take authority over the devil and his attacks.

By recognizing that God has given you power over emotional attacks, you can overcome every tactic of the enemy and prevent him from blocking your destiny. Open your mouth, release your faith, and declare the Word of God over your life. Become emotionally invincible by using God's Word to seize your destiny.

Foundation Scripture

Behold, I give unto you power to tread on serpents and scorpions, and over all the power of the enemy: and nothing shall by any means hurt you.

Luke 10:19

Practical Application

You have authority over every negative emotion that arises in your life. Begin exercising your authority over these feelings by aggressively speaking God's Word *every* time the enemy attacks you with depression, fear, rejection, or anxiety. There is power in what you say, so schedule time daily to confess the Word over emotions.

Get a Grip!

Have you ever had the feeling that the things going on in your life are out of control? Maybe you got into an argument with someone and in the heat of the moment said or did something you later regretted. We have all experienced those situations at one time or another. Just think about a time when you were stuck in traffic on a sweltering, hot day, or maybe in a long line at the grocery store—and maybe it was the cashier's first day on the job. Highly irritating situations wear down your tolerance, but you can take control over your emotions.

God designed you to express yourself through emotions. Your feelings can lead you to show compassion toward others. Because Jesus had feelings, He was able to relate to mankind and identify with daily life experiences. However, Jesus maintained control over His emotions and never allowed them to control Him. Jesus never allowed His emotions to cause hurt or pain to someone else. While He did express righteous indignation at the temple, His emotions caused Him to respond positively. As a result, people were healed, set free, and delivered.

God designed you to express yourself through emotions.

HOW EMOTIONS BECAME PERVERTED

Before Adam sinned in the Garden of Eden by eating of the Tree of the Knowledge of Good and Evil, his mind, will, and emotions were perfectly aligned with those of the Father. When sin entered his heart through disobedience, the curse entered the Earth and caused a separation in Adam's relationship with his heavenly Father. As a result, mankind became subjected to the curse of being emotionally ruled.

MEN AND WOMEN: EMOTIONAL MYTHS OR TRUTH?

Women are often considered highly emotional—more emotional than men. While there may be some truth to that, it certainly doesn't apply to every individual. Everyone can train his or her emotions to line up with God's Word.

When it comes to gender differences, it is important to look at how boys and girls are socially identified from a very young age. Boys are taught to hide their emotions, because emotional outbursts are considered a sign of weakness. Consequently, many boys grow up to be incapable of showing the natural, human side of their emotions. On the other hand, many girls are often taught to be open with their feelings and to verbally express them.

While some differences are based on training, men and women do experience and process their emotions in different ways. Women tend to be more aware of their emotions and able to express them. Many times they know what they are feeling and why, whereas men aren't always sure what they feel. Men may even mislabel their feelings. For example, many men think they're experiencing anger when they're actually feeling fearful about something in their lives. I've experienced that myself. Once I became angry with Taffi about a business issue, and I had to ask myself why I was so angry. After an in-depth self-evaluation, the Lord revealed to me that it was fear that caused me to respond the way I did.

Another important thing to remember is that men often don't reveal their emotions. A man may be dealing with serious emotional issues in his life, but in an attempt to show that he is "keeping it all together," he may repress the outward expression of what he is really feeling. If emotions aren't released or dealt with constructively, they will surface in other ways, often in destructive or hurtful ways toward others. Men have been conditioned to believe things like "men don't cry," yet that is so far from the truth. Crying or not crying has nothing to do with masculinity. Crying releases emotions that are built up on the inside. The Word of God is the only way to successfully manage your emotions.

The Word of God is the only way to successfully manage your emotions.

CONTROL YOUR EMOTIONS

If you want to dig to the very root issue of emotions, you have to deal with how you think. The way you think governs the emotions that follow. If you think it is okay to be verbally abusive to someone every time they do something that hurts you, then you will carry that action out. If you think it's okay to have sex outside of marriage, then when a tempting situation faces you, your feelings will lead you to do something you will later regret. If you allow your emotions to control you and move you in a negative direction, you are going to find yourself wondering, *How did I get here?* The answer is simple—your emotions took you there. You didn't make sound decisions because you were driven by how you felt at the moment. You made decisions based on your emotions.

Just because you are thinking about or feeling something doesn't mean you have to give attention to it or act on it. When you exercise self-control, you are controlling your emotions as an act of your own will. You are literally saying, "No, I refuse to feel that way. I refuse to think that thought." You cast down wrong thoughts, imaginations, and feelings by speaking the Word of God over them.

Proverbs 16:32 says, "He that is slow to anger is better than the mighty; and he that ruleth his spirit than he that taketh a city." According to the Hebrew translation of this Scripture, the word "spirit" refers to the soul. This Scripture says the person who has control over his emotions is more powerful than an army that takes a city!

In contrast, if a person is under the control of his emotions, he can be easily overtaken by the enemy. This is why getting our emotions under control is so vital. Christians have no business being manipulated by the devil.

USE YOUR AUTHORITY

So many people are out of the will of God for their lives because they allowed their emotions to lead them in the wrong direction. This happens when we allow offense, anger, or depression to go unchecked. Indulging those unhealthy feelings gives Satan the opportunity to begin controlling your life, causing you to make bad decisions.

But take heart! God has given you authority over your emotions. They shouldn't, under any circumstances, control you. You can refuse to be at their mercy. The next time you are tempted to yield to negative emotions, ask yourself what big accomplishment the devil might be trying to prevent you from achieving. Where is he trying to lead you? You can be sure it is out of the will of God. Why are those emotions there in the first place? What have you been meditating on and thinking about? Go to the Word, find Scriptures that deal with your situation, and start speaking them. Declare the promises of God over your life, and cast down every thought and feeling that opposes the Word. Remind yourself that God has freed you from the power of negative emotions.

Do what Jesus did. In the midst of a highly emotional situation in the Garden of Gethsemane, He prayed and kept moving forward. That's exactly what you must do. When your bills are due and it seems as if you are running out of resources, don't panic. Instead, declare the Word of God. Doing so will get your feelings back under control.

In addition, talk to God when you feel emotionally under attack. He is always available and wants to help you. He loves you and desires that you walk victoriously over the pressures of life. Talk to Him when fear strikes you, or when you are hit by discouragement or depression. Let Him know how you really feel. When you release those feelings to Him and trust Him to get involved in your situation, you will begin to experience the peace that passes all understanding.

Trusting in God and His Word will deliver you from stress and emotional attacks. By exercising your God-given authority over your feelings, you can experience total freedom from negative emotions. The decision is yours—to live an emotion-ruled life or a God-ruled life. By choosing the latter, you can rest assured that you will make the right decisions and ultimately experience the good life God has predestined for you.

> *By exercising your God-given authority over your feelings, you can experience total freedom from negative emotions.*

Review Nuggets

Emotions move you in a certain direction—either toward or away from the will of God for your life. God designed you to have emotions, but He never intended for your emotions to control you. Follow Jesus' example by praying and continuing to move forward toward what God has called you to do. Trust God to hold true to His Word and give you total victory over your emotions, so that you are no longer bound and controlled by them. Take authority by speaking the Word and declaring what God has already promised you about your situation.

Foundation Scripture

For we do not have a High Priest Who is unable to understand and sympathize and have a shared feeling with our weaknesses and infirmities and liability to the assaults of temptation, but One Who has been tempted in every respect as we are, yet without sinning.

Hebrews 4:15 (AMP)

Practical Application

Whether you are male or female, you *can* control your emotions. Refuse to entertain negative thoughts and wrong imaginations by speaking the Word of God when those thoughts and imaginations try to enter your mind. If you find yourself in an emotionally charged environment, pray, and continue to move forward. Find Scriptures that deal with your situation and meditate on them until your life moves from being emotionally-ruled to God-ruled.

Step 4

Make Powerful
Decisions

7 *Steps to a Quality Decision*

You are a person of destiny. God has a specific plan for your life! Before the foundation of the world, He chose you to live at this particular time. Regardless of what you may have been told, you are not a mistake—God knew you before you were ever formed in your mother's womb (Jeremiah 1:5). He made you with a purpose, and you are a vital part of His divine plan to bring more people into the Kingdom of God. In order to fulfill your God-given purpose, you must be mindful of the choices you make, and refuse to be led by your emotions. Quality decisions based on God's Word will place you on the right path. However, bad choices will take you off course and prevent you from experiencing God's best.

You are a free moral agent; you have a right to make your own decisions. God won't *make* you do anything! No, He has given you the ability to make your own decisions. *You* determine your level of success or failure by making decisions that either line up with His Word or go against it. *You* determine your level of success or failure. If you are not where you want to be in life, don't blame the devil or God. Your current station in life is the result of the choices *you've* made.

You *determine your level of success or failure.*

As a pastor, it is my responsibility to ensure that my congregation understands God's Word. I make the Scriptures plain so they can clearly understand what God is saying. Once they understand, they have to make a decision. They must decide to believe that the Word is true and that they can be, have, and possess all that is written therein. Every Believer must choose to make what God says in His Word the final authority for his or her life. That is the only way the Word becomes a reality.

Hebrews 11:24–26 says:

> By faith Moses, when he was come to years, refused to be called the son of Pharaoh's daughter; Choosing rather to suffer affliction with the people of God, than to enjoy the pleasures of sin for a season; Esteeming the reproach of Christ greater riches than the treasures in Egypt: for he had respect unto the recompence of the reward.

Notice three powerful words in that Scripture: *refused, choosing,* and *esteeming.* Let's examine these words more closely in terms of how they relate to your decisions.

START THE PROCESS

There are seven steps for making quality decisions. The process begins with three steps: esteeming, refusing, and choosing. Let's look at the first word, *esteeming.* To esteem something is to "give it weight or value." When you esteem something, you judge, measure, balance, and weigh it carefully; you hold it in high regard. In Hebrews 11:26, we learn that Moses *esteemed* the reproach of Christ of greater value than the treasures in Egypt. In other words, he placed a higher value on suffering with his people than enjoying the pleasures available to him as the adopted son of Pharaoh's daughter. He knew the will of God for his life would afford him far greater riches.

In your decision-making process, you must first assign value to your choices. What carries the most weight? Is pleasing God more important than pleasing others? God's approval should be more valuable to you than looking good in the eyes of your friends, family, or acquaintances. Consider these things when making decisions. It could drastically affect the course of your life.

When I was a child, I used to play on the seesaw on the playground. The balance of the seesaw is in the middle. If there are equal weights on each side, it stays level. However, if the weight on one side is heavier, the other side rises up in the air. Likewise, when you place your decisions on a mental seesaw, they may start out balanced, but once you start to weigh, judge, and measure, you will notice that one side will begin to outweigh the other.

You must ask yourself this very important question: "How much value does the Word of God have in my life?" You will not make quality decisions until you value God's Word. If His Word doesn't have value in your life, you will make worldly, even sinful, decisions.

Many Christians do not esteem the Word of God. Instead, they esteem the words of talk-show hosts, psychologists, and the media. It should be no surprise that their decisions aren't yielding the desired results. The good news is, you can avoid the consequences of making poor choices by esteeming God's Word above every other influence in your life.

You can avoid the consequences of making poor choices by esteeming God's Word above every other influence in your life.

Every decision you make must be measured by the Word of God. It must become your final authority. It must be the basis for your marriage, parenting, finances, employment, residence, and church home. If the Word of God isn't the final authority, you don't have a foundation to stand on. Ask yourself, "Have I made the Word my final authority?" You haven't settled this issue if you are still arguing with the Word, questioning it, and choosing the world's ways over God's. All questions cease when you make the Word your final authority.

Steps two and three for making quality decisions are to *refuse* and *choose* respectively. To refuse means "to deny, denounce, reject or disown." In Hebrews 11:24, Moses *refused* to be called the son of Pharaoh's daughter. He denounced his position as a member of the royal family so he could pursue the will of God. He could no longer sit quietly and watch the injustice and oppression his people suffered at the hands of the Egyptians. It was his refusal to stay connected to Israel's oppressors that enabled him to take the next step: *choosing* to suffer affliction with the people of God rather than enjoying the pleasures of sin for a season (Hebrews 11:25). Moses made a quality decision that ultimately led to the freedom of more than two million people.

If you are in debt or experiencing lack, sickness, or disease, you must first *refuse* to accept those negative circumstances and then *choose* to be free from them. When was the last time you looked at your bills and said, "I denounce debt?" When was the last time you denounced sickness and lack in your life? I'm not suggesting you pretend these things don't exist. I am saying you can refuse to accept them when they show up.

Think about trying to feed a baby something he doesn't want to eat. He will spit out every spoonful you put in his mouth. That's his way of refusing it. When it comes to the attacks of the devil, Christians must respond like a baby who stubbornly refuses to eat food he doesn't like. Refuse everything that doesn't line up with the Word of God, and choose those things that bring peace, wholeness, and happiness into your life.

ACTION STEPS

After completing the first part of the process—esteeming, refusing, and choosing—you need to continue on the path to making a quality decision. Many people take the initial steps but fail to complete the process. There are four action steps you need to take to complete the process of making a quality decision. Your decision is not and will not become one of quality if you fail to complete all four action steps.

Hebrews 11:27–29 says:

By faith he forsook Egypt, not fearing the wrath of the king: for he endured, as seeing him who is invisible. Through faith he kept the passover, and the sprinkling of blood, lest he that destroyed the firstborn should touch them. By faith they passed through the

Red sea as by dry land: which the Egyptians assaying to do were drowned.

Once Moses started the process by refusing, choosing, and esteeming, he then took four action steps: he forsook, endured, kept, and passed through. And that is exactly what you must do.

1. To *forsake* means to "leave something behind." Moses forsook Egypt, which represented bondage and the world's system. In other words, he left the bondage of the world's system behind. Are you willing to forsake the things that are holding you in bondage? They may be habits, attitudes, or relationships. Only you know those areas of your life that are a hindrance to your spiritual growth and relationship with God. Whatever they are, if you want to set yourself on the path to your destiny, you've got to forsake them.

For example, to forsake smoking, you must be willing to do what it takes to leave that addictive habit behind. If you want to lose ten pounds, you must be willing to exercise and turn away from high-calorie desserts, fried foods, and sugar. You must leave the old things behind and start doing what you've purposed in your heart. Refusing requires thought, but forsaking requires action.

The number-one obstacle to taking action is fear. When you give in to fear and imagine that you will fail, you've stopped the process. Feelings of inadequacy and memories of past failures are other obstacles to stepping out and acting on your quality decision. To make progress, you must be confident in your ability to succeed. With God on your side, and Heaven backing your decision, your success is guaranteed. It's just a matter of believing it for yourself.

> *With God on your side, and Heaven backing your decision, your success is guaranteed. It's just a matter of believing it for yourself.*

I remember when God first spoke to me about starting this ministry. I was filled with anxiety and feelings of inadequacy. In fact, I was terrified! One evening I pulled my car over to the side of the road. At the time, I didn't know what an anxiety attack was, but I know now I was having one. I thought I was dying right there in my car! I had made a decision to go forward with the vision God had given me. Then I began thinking about everything involved, and fear entered my mind. I had to address that fear by casting it out of my thoughts and pressing on with my decision to obey God. I followed up on my decision, and with the necessary action, World Changers Church International became a reality, and lives are being changed all over the world.

2. The next action step is to endure. To *endure* is to "carry something through to completion"; to hang in there until you see the results you believe will come. According to the online resource blueletterbible. com, the word *endurance* in Greek means "to be strong, steadfast, and patient." The Latin definition is "to harden like steel." Once you've forsaken things that will hinder you from fulfilling your destiny, it is time to become hard like steel. That is necessary in order to make it through the challenges that will come your way. Once you've made your decision, plant your feet and don't allow anything or anyone to move you.

Several years ago, I made a decision to lose some weight. I was tired of looking like I was five months pregnant. One day Taffi took a donut and put it right under my nose. What a temptation! I remember shaking and having to call on the Lord to help me in that moment! But no matter how badly I wanted to eat that donut, I didn't give in to the temptation. I was like steel; Taffi was amazed. As a matter of fact, *I* was amazed! My endurance enabled me to be victorious.

Back when I was conducting campus ministry in college, I received a prophecy that enabled me to endure. I was new to the ministry and was facing some challenges as I dealt with the different attitudes and personalities of people around me. One night when I was extremely tired, a man came up to me and said, "I had a vision. In it I saw your backbone hardening like steel. People hit it, but it wouldn't move. You've been tested, and now you have a backbone of steel." That really encouraged me. No matter what I had to experience from week to week, I kept going. I refused to allow anyone to prevent me from fulfilling God's will for my life.

3. Hebrews 11:28 says, "Through faith he kept the passover, and the sprinkling of blood, lest he that destroyed the firstborn should touch them." Moses kept the Passover. So what does that mean for you? Continue doing what you already know to do. Regardless of your situation, obey God, and He will help you walk out the quality decision you have made.

For example, you know that if you want to get out of debt, you're going to have to change your spending habits. You cannot continue spending beyond your means and buying things on credit. You know what you need to do. Now keep on doing it!

4. The final action step is to pass through. Isaiah 43:2-3 says:

When thou passest through the waters, I will be with thee; and through the rivers, they shall not overflow thee: when thou walkest through the fire, thou shalt not be burned; neither shall the flame kindle upon thee. For I am the LORD thy God, the Holy One of Israel, thy Saviour: I gave Egypt for thy ransom.

Isn't it wonderful to know God is with you as you pass through everything that tries to hinder your quality decisions? When you feel like quitting, go back to the Word of God. Have confidence. Your heavenly Father is right there with you. He will support you in making decisions that are in line with His Word and His will.

Review Nuggets

There are several steps you must take to make lasting quality decisions: *esteem* the Word, *refuse* that which opposes the Word, and *choose* God's way over your way or the world's way. Once you've done those things, take action by forsaking anything that might hinder your goal. Endure the hard times and challenges that come your way, and continue to do what you already know to do until you finally pass through to victory! As you follow these steps, you will find yourself walking in the will of God for your life.

Foundation Scripture

By faith Moses, when he was come to years, refused to be called the son of Pharaoh's daughter; Choosing rather to suffer affliction with the people of God, than to enjoy the pleasures of sin for a season; Esteeming the reproach of Christ greater riches than the treasures in Egypt: for he had respect unto the recompence of the reward.

Hebrews 11:24–26

Practical Application

Reread the steps to a quality decision, and write them down in your journal. Apply these steps to a specific situation in your life. Write down the things you experience as you apply each step to your circumstance. As you take steps toward victory, chart how your situation turns around.

Growth Produces Change

You've probably heard the cliché that change is inevitable, but desiring to change and actually going through the change process are quite different. Arriving at the destination God has for you will require growing in the knowledge and understanding of His Word. In a June 24, 1963, speech to political notables at the Paulskirche in Frankfurt, Germany, John F. Kennedy said: "Change is the law of life. And those who look only to the past or present are certain to miss the future." In a spiritual sense, holding on to your old way of thinking will cause you to miss out on what God has planned for your future! As you make a conscious effort to grow spiritually through His Word, you will notice a positive change in your reactions, your thought life, and the decisions you make. Positive change is a result of growth. If you aren't seeing change in your life, it may be that your spiritual growth has become stagnant.

Here's what I mean. If you've been a member of a church for years, but you have the same bad attitude you've always had, there's been no growth. If you are still offended by things that offended you years ago, there's been no growth. To get different results, you must make a decision to do things differently. Apply the Word of God, and allow Him to strengthen you.

To get different results, you must make a decision to do things differently.

UNDERSTAND THE PROCESS

Spiritual growth starts when you are born again. At that point, you become a child of God, and your growth process as His son or daughter begins. Galatians 4:1, 2 says, "Now I say, That the heir, as long as he is a child, differeth nothing from a servant, though he be lord of all; But is under tutors and governors until the time appointed of the father." Notice that although you have an inheritance as a child of God, you access it by growing in relationship as His son or daughter and reaching spiritual maturity.

HAS YOUR GROWTH STAGNATED?

Something exciting happens when your spirit is born again: your old nature dies, and you are recreated with a new spiritual nature. You will notice that the way you do things is different. You now have authority over addictions, depression, fear, and sickness through the Word of God.

Although the born-again experience takes place in your spirit, your mind must be renewed as an act of your will. Mind renewal is a gradual process that continues as you walk with the Lord. As you fellowship with God and study His Word, you will have success. However, if you aren't experiencing growth and noticing changes in the way you think, act, or speak, you may have hit an obstacle that needs to be identified and dealt with. Let's explore a few of those obstacles.

OBSTACLES TO GROWTH

1. Lack of discipline.

One reason you may experience stunted spiritual growth is a lack of discipline. Discipline takes determination and will require you to do things that may be difficult or uncomfortable. Discipline requires you to do what is necessary to achieve the results you desire.

I remember a minister's conference Taffi and I went to. I was up all night in prayer and was really seeking direction from God. I remember praying, "Lord, say something to me, please." I prayed and waited all night because I needed to hear from Him. At the conference the next day, I was very sleepy. Nothing the speaker said made sense to me. I was so tired that my vision was blurred to the point that I saw duplicates of the speaker! I even drifted a few times and had to look around to remember where I was. All of a sudden, I had a little talk with myself and said, "Sit up. Take notes. Listen to what the speaker is saying. Do what you have to do to understand, and you will be all right!" I had to exercise discipline to get what I needed that night. It was for my benefit—I needed growth in my life.

2. Inconsistent prayer life.

You can also stagnate your spiritual growth by not establishing a consistent prayer life. Knowing how to go to God in prayer regarding challenging situations in your life will move Him to work on your behalf. You must be disciplined to consistently seek God in prayer—not only to speak to Him, but to listen to Him as well. Sometimes people talk themselves out of developing an effective prayer life because they don't feel it's a necessity, but it is! Nothing will happen on Earth until someone goes before the Lord in prayer, because prayer provokes action in the heavenly realm.

3. Failure to set up proper boundaries.

While it is important to make a decision, the most important part of your decision is the boundaries you set up around it. Your success will be determined by your boundaries. For example, if you have quit smoking, you must place boundaries around that decision. This may mean avoiding the stores where you are likely to purchase tobacco products. It may also mean avoiding being around others who smoke.

Ask yourself the following questions to determine your growth level:

- Am I dealing with the same issues I dealt with when I was first born again?
- Is it easier for me to walk in love toward others now than when I first accepted Jesus as Lord of my life?
- Has my conversation changed? Does my speech line up with God's Word?
- Am I quick to obey God when He directs me to do something?
- Do I disagree with the Word about issues or behaviors I refuse to change? Do I use repentance as an excuse to sin, knowing I can ask for forgiveness later?
- Do I make excuses for my behavior instead of making a quality decision to change?
- Do I have the ability to honestly evaluate myself, or do others have to tell me?
- Are my decisions in line with the Word of God?
- Do I hear God clearly, and is the clarity of my hearing evidenced by the decisions I make?
- Do I still have the same tolerance level toward ungodliness that I did when I first made Jesus Lord of my life?

These questions are not the end-all means to determining your level of spiritual growth, but they are signposts to get you thinking about where you are and where you're going. When you answer these questions honestly, you can adjust areas where growth is needed to be successful in your walk with God.

Numbers 32:23 says if you aren't doing what God has instructed you to do, it is sin. It states further that your sin will find you out. In other words, the sin will be exposed. You will not reach the next level with God if there are areas of sin that you are holding on to.

Is your love walk pleasing to God? In Matthew 22:37–40, Jesus lets us know that loving God and loving others are the two greatest commandments. As you progress as a Christian, growth in this area should be evident. This is not to say that you won't face negative emotions at times, but the key is to deal with them when they surface.

Look at yourself from God's perspective to see if change has truly taken place. Remember that growth equals change, and change comes when you consistently apply the principles of God's Word to your life.

> *Growth equals change, and change comes when you consistently apply the principles of God's Word to your life.*

GOD, I WANT TO CHANGE!

Change will not happen as a result of your ability or will. You must decide that you want to change, and through the power of God's Word, you can. He is available to strengthen you in your walk so you can experience dramatic growth and change. Your heavenly Father understands that you may stumble along the way and even have to repeat a few lessons, but as a spiritual parent, He is there to help you make it through. He understands that the growth process must take place in order for you to go to the next level.

The apostle Paul wrote that when he was a child, he did childish things, but he went on to say that as he matured, he grew out of his childish ways (1 Corinthians 13:11). God understands your desire to change and will empower you to succeed in this area. With His help, you will accomplish far more than you could ever imagine. Take the necessary steps to grow and mature in your relationship with Him.

Review Nuggets

The evidence that spiritual growth and maturity have taken place in your life is noticeable change—change in your actions, speech, thoughts, and way of doing things. It takes making a quality decision to implement change. Evaluate your growth, identify areas where you may have become stagnant, and make the necessary changes for improvement. Create a life that is strong in prayer, seeking God through His Word and through fellowship. Continue to grow in God's Word and experience His success!

Foundation Scripture

I call heaven and earth to record this day against you, that I have set before you life and death, blessing and cursing: therefore choose life, that both thou and thy seed may live.

Deuteronomy 30:19

Practical Application

Make the decision: Take an honest look at your spiritual growth, and identify the areas of your life you have not completely surrendered to God. There may be a behavior, attitude, or habit that is hard for you to release. Recognize that in order to go to the next level with God, you must change. Write those challenges down in your journal, and take them before the Lord. Get a concordance and look up Scriptures that offer solutions in those areas. Ask God to show you practical things you can do to overcome them.

Step 5

Evaluate Your Actions

Check Yourself: Your Actions Have Power!

To create a lifestyle that is aligned with God's Word, this fifth step is vital. This step will lead you to take actions that work to your advantage. Actions that line up with God's Word will produce step six—establishing habits that line up with God's Word. Habits that line up with God's Word will lead you to step seven—developing character that lines up with God's Word. Together, these steps will lead you to the victorious destiny God has for you.

Taking right actions (actions that line up with the Word of God) must be preceded by right words, thinking, emotions, and decisions. If you speak wrong words, have wrong thinking, and make wrong decisions, you will take wrong actions. In William Shakespeare's play *Hamlet*, Hamlet remarks, "Suit the action to the word, the word to the action." Ultimately your actions speak far louder than your words.

In James 1:22 we are encouraged to be doers of the Word and not just hearers. As a pastor, I see and talk to a lot of people every day. It's disheartening to see people come to church, receive a needed answer to a problem, hear and understand the Word God has for them, and then go home and fail to act on what they've heard. This is what the Bible refers to when it says you deceive yourself if you *hear* the Word and fail to *do* it (James 1:22). Your actions have the potential to catapult you to prosperity or poverty. The results you need won't come just by hearing the Word; you must act on what you hear!

WHY YOU DO WHAT YOU DO

I always say, nothing just happens. People don't just behave the way they do for no reason. Our actions are shaped by our thoughts, feelings, and decisions. This is why it's necessary for the Word to be our foundation.

If you were raised in a family that embraced revenge, it is likely an action that characterizes your behavior today. Ask yourself, "Do my actions honor God?" God's Word should weigh more heavily in your life than the opinions and words of others. Your actions will either honor or dishonor God.

GOD'S WATCHFUL EYES

How can you make sure your actions are favorable in God's sight? Obey the Word of God, and search your heart regularly to make sure your motives are pure. A heart that is pure is the source of actions that are in line with God's Word.

First Samuel 1:20–28 tells the story of Hannah, who believed God for the supernatural birth of a son. She vowed to God that if He gave her a son, she would give him back to God. The Bible says she prayed an earnest, heartfelt prayer, and God heard her and gave her the son she desired. She kept her word and dedicated him to the Lord.

Hannah's story is a prime illustration of how our actions hold weight with God. During the celebration of her son's birth, Hannah said, "Talk no more so exceeding proudly; let not arrogancy come out of your mouth: for the LORD is a God of knowledge, and by him actions are weighed" (1 Samuel 2:3). Hannah acknowledged that God considers the motives behind actions and words.

Are your motives pure and solidly based on God's Word and the leading of His Spirit, or are they the result of your own selfish desires and self-will? God's watchful eyes are ever considering your actions and the motives behind them. While people are busy looking at your outward appearance only, God is very interested in what's going on inside your heart as well. "But the LORD said unto Samuel, Look not on his countenance, or on the height of his stature; because I have refused him: for the LORD seeth not as man seeth; for man looketh on the outward appearance, but the LORD looketh on the heart" (1 Samuel 16:7). Pure motives and corresponding action will put you on, and keep you on, the path to your destiny.

WHAT'S LOVE GOT TO DO WITH IT? EVERYTHING!

If you are wondering how to experience God's favor all the time, make a decision to consistently demonstrate the love of God toward others. Regardless of the situation or how you are treated, when you operate from a position of unconditional love, the blessings of God can't help but show up in your life. What you do for the benefit of others has a direct effect on what God does in *your* life.

> *What you do for the benefit of others has a direct effect on what God does in your life.*

God approves actions that are driven by love. You may think it is impossible to love others unconditionally, or do something positive for someone who has done you wrong, but that's not true. If you are a Believer, you possess God's supernatural ability to love. This ability was deposited in your heart by way of the Holy Spirit the day you invited Christ into your heart (Romans 5:5). God has made it possible for you to do the impossible—to love and do good to those who are unlovable, or who have hurt you.

Walking in love carries great rewards. It is easy to be nice to people who are kind to you, and it is true that any act of love honors God; but God particularly values our love for those who are difficult to love. This is where the God-kind of love kicks in and allows you to sow what I call the "do-good seed." When you sow seeds of love in unfriendly soil, you reap an immense reward. God smiles on such actions because they demonstrate true devotion to His Word (Ephesians 5:1).

Love is the most powerful weapon we possess. It paralyzes the devil and flushes out fear. In Mark 12:30, 31, Jesus said that the two most important commandments are to love God with all your heart, mind, soul, and strength and to love your neighbor as yourself. *Everything* hangs on the law of love, including prosperity in every area of our lives.

Everything hangs on the law of love, including prosperity in every area of our lives.

In Luke 6:27, Jesus says, "But I say unto you which hear, Love your enemies, do good to them which hate you." God is telling you that love is the way to handle those who come against you. Take every opportunity to reflect God's love to others, even when it's difficult. Doing so will open the door for God to bless you abundantly.

Pray for those who spread lies about you, steal from you, or betray you. Give to someone in need, even if that person has hurt you in the past. Reach out to someone who may not deserve it. Your acts of kindness *will* be rewarded.

When your decisions are based upon the love of God and His Word, your actions will put you on the path to success. As a result, your character and ultimate destination will be in line with the will of God.

Acting in love will change you and every relationship you have! Something awesome happens when you do things out of love, especially toward those who have wronged or upset you. God is love, and every time you demonstrate love, you demonstrate your connection to Him and it becomes an example of His character to those around you. Your loving actions guarantee that God will act on your behalf!

Review Nuggets

It is vital to be not only a hearer of the Word, but also a doer (James 1:22). God weighs your actions and your motives. When you act in love toward someone who has hurt you, you demonstrate the character of God and open the door for Him to act on your behalf. Your decision to act in love will impact others and even spark change in their lives.

Walking in love must be the foundation for everything you do. Examine your heart. When opportunities to sow do-good seeds arise, take advantage of them. Then you can expect to receive a good harvest. Position yourself for success and the abundant life by allowing your actions to be motivated by love.

Foundation Scripture

Therefore all things whatsoever ye would that men should do to you, do ye even so to them: for this is the law and the prophets.

Matthew 7:12

Practical Application

Walking in love is sometimes challenging, especially when someone has done something hurtful and unkind to you. However, in order to experience the abundant life that God has predestined for you, you must act in love. Be a hearer and a doer of God's Word. Make a list of people you feel have hurt you, and commit to pray for them fervently for the next twenty-one days. Find Scriptures that deal with praying for your enemies, and meditate on them. Speak blessings daily over the unlovable people in your life. Write down how your prayers change your attitude toward them.

As you are faithful to love your enemies, you will notice something powerful happening in your heart. You will begin to feel the love of God toward them. If He reveals to you the root to their behavior, purpose in your heart to pray for them even more. Have confidence that you are impacting someone else's life through your prayers and are overcoming your own selfishness in the process. Your harvest will be a great one!

The Boomerang Effect

Have you heard the saying, "What goes around, comes around"? Maybe you didn't know it when you heard it, but this familiar phrase is based on a biblical principle. While some people call it karma or the universe's way of balancing things, the truth is, it is a spiritual law that, when put into motion, will work for anyone who uses it.

The Bible says, "Be not deceived; God is not mocked: for whatsoever a man soweth, that shall he also reap" (Galatians 6:7). The law of seedtime and harvest will always produce *something*, either good or bad. The types of seeds you sow, whether in word or deed, will produce a boomerang effect of blessings or consequences.

Genesis 8:22 says, "While the earth remaineth, seedtime and harvest, and cold and heat, and summer and winter, and day and night shall not cease." Whether you are a Christian or not, you can't avoid the effects of sowing and reaping. In fact, God says this process is guaranteed, just like cold and heat, summer and winter, day and night.

Everything you do, whether good or bad, will come back to you. That may be a scary thought as you evaluate the seeds you've sown recently, but if you recognize that you've set the law into motion with the wrong actions, you can change the outcome by repenting and replacing wrong actions with good ones as you move forward.

DO THE RIGHT THINGS

Walking in love is the number-one priority of every Believer. When your actions are governed by love, you can be confident that you will like what you reap. Doing the right thing is doing the *love* thing. It is the God thing to do.

Look at Galatians 5:22, 23, which describes the fruit of the Spirit. It says, "But the fruit of the Spirit is love, joy, peace, longsuffering, gentleness, goodness, faith, Meekness, temperance: against such there is no law." This is your action guideline for doing the right things in life. When you are about to do something, ask yourself, is this going to demonstrate love, joy, peace, or patience? Is it a reflection of gentleness, goodness, faith, meekness, and temperance? You can't go wrong if your actions express these attributes.

As soon as you immerse yourself in the process of becoming more Christ-like through your words and actions, you will be tested. Satan will try to convince you that there is no point in your effort—that it won't produce the results you want. His goal is to undermine your efforts to walk in love and try to keep you from your destiny. He will tempt you to question why you are walking in love by disturbing your emotions, offending you, or frustrating you in some way. Despite his efforts, don't give in. God's way is always the best and most perfect way.

God's way is always the best and most perfect way.

SOW A DO-GOOD SEED

I have had many opportunities to do the opposite of love in various situations. I remember a particularly challenging moment when I was tested in this area. I had gone to the movies with Taffi, and we were sitting in the theater. During that time in my life, I had made a decision to drink eight ounces of water every thirty minutes, so I opened my cell phone to check whether it was time for my next water break.

All of a sudden I felt someone behind me tapping me hard on my shoulder. "Excuse me!" he said. I guess he was irritated because the light from my cell phone was shining and was distracting him from watching the movie. Irritated and bordering on being highly offended, I replied, "What?" The audacity of a complete stranger to practically hit me on my shoulder and rudely bark at me in the theater really ticked me off!

Then the Spirit of God spoke to me saying, "Don't say another word. Don't say anything else, because anything that comes out of your mouth at this point will take you out of love and to a place you don't want to go." Immediately I knew I had to get my emotions under control or someone was going to catch the backhand of the anointing, if you know what I mean!

Selfishness and the love of God warred for control of my mind. It was as if the devil was saying, "What are you going to do now, Cref? Are you going to let this complete stranger talk to you like that?" Selfishness was talking to me that day and it said, "Beat the snot out of this guy!"

About forty-five minutes passed, and I was still distracted. Selfishness was saying, "You need to do something." I couldn't even focus on the movie because I was trying to figure out a safe way to get revenge! I considered getting my phone out again and opening it up so the light could annoy the man again, but then God spoke to me again, saying, "You will be out of My love if you do that." He said, "You don't have to know the guy to walk in love." I had to make a decision to either walk in love or indulge my desire for revenge.

Taffi tapped me on the leg and said, "It's easier to preach it than to go through the test, isn't it?" She was right; it *was* easier. But I made the decision to walk in love that day by refusing to respond with negative actions. This was my do-good seed. I might not have seen the harvest right away, but the seed was sown.

That's what sowing a love seed through a love action is about. You may not see the results immediately, but you can be certain God sees your heart and will honor your decision to obey His commandment to love.

Why does God require you to respond in love rather than retaliate in selfishness? Why does He ask you to sow a do-good seed, even when doing so makes you feel like the loser in the situation? God *is* love

(1 John 4:8), and as His representative on the Earth, you must demonstrate His character through your actions. The world makes love seem weak, but it is only through love that you walk in the authority that God has given you.

> *The world makes love seem weak, but it is only through love that you walk in the authority that God has given you.*

BUILD JUDGMENT INTO THE ACTION

It is easy to blame God or the devil when things don't seem to be going well in your life, but many times the responsibility lies with your own actions. If you act in line with God's Spirit, the outcome will be abundant life, but if you act outside of love, in line with the law of sin and death, the result will be destruction.

Despite what some may tell you, God is not out to punish you or make you suffer. The enemy wants you to go through Hell on Earth and will try everything he can to seduce you into operating according to his system. If your thinking, emotions, and decisions are not submitted to the Word of God, you will take the wrong actions, which will ultimately destroy your life. That's not God's fault; it's spiritual law.

The good news is, you can take control of your life. If you realize you've gotten off the path to the good life, turn around! It's just like going south on a highway when you want to go north. If you keep passing the exit signs, you'll never turn around. God loves you so much that He will give you signs and clues on the road of life to help get you back on the right path. It is your responsibility to recognize them and act on what He shows you to get yourself going in the right direction.

Your actions are seeds that will produce a harvest in your life. You want to make sure the results of what you sow are peace, prosperity, abundance, and love. For this reason, it is critical that you constantly evaluate your heart and your actions.

The Bible says when you judge yourself, you won't be judged (1 Corinthians 11:31). Why wait until your actions come back to haunt you? Take time each day to judge yourself. Ask God, "Lord, did I do anything today that wasn't motivated by love?" Or, "You know what, Lord? When I said that to So-and-So, it wasn't coming from a heart of love. My motives weren't pure. I was really angry with her about what she did a couple of weeks ago. Forgive me." This type of self-evaluation isn't always easy, but it will help you. God appreciates when you are honest with yourself and Him.

Allow the Holy Spirit to lead you in everything you do. He will quicken you in your spirit when your actions are not godly. You will feel uneasy about whatever you've done or are getting ready to do or say. Don't ignore that feeling. It is God's way of keeping you on the right path.

If you've already missed the mark in an area, repent! Don't give the negative effects of your actions time to manifest in your life. Quickly go to God when you realize what you've done and confess to Him with a sincere heart. When you ask Him to forgive you, He is faithful. Be open to receive His loving correction for your actions.

ACHIEVE YOUR GOOD LIFE THROUGH GOD'S SYSTEM

One day I asked the Lord why it was necessary to sow seeds. He said, "It is the only way I can get involved in your situation. Seedtime and harvest are my way of helping you reach the good life."

When you understand this, it becomes clear why sowing good seeds through the right actions is so critical. Operating in line with the system God has set up guarantees the right results. When you love your enemies, you are sowing a do-good seed and operating spiritual laws to your advantage. If you do something kind for someone, and demonstrate the fruit of the Spirit, you have the edge. On the flip side, if someone does something bad to you and you return negativity to them, you will only reap more of the same.

God doesn't want hate or any other attack of the devil to boomerang on you, so do the right thing! Your do-good seeds are more powerful than Satan. Good will always overcome evil.

Good will always overcome evil.

Keep in mind that God will protect your free will. He will protect it all the way to Hell if you decide to go there—but that doesn't have to be your final destination. Get in the Bible and meditate on the character of God. Check out Jesus' actions. He was always sowing seeds of love. Even in death, sowing Himself as the ultimate sacrifice, He reaped a harvest of Christians who will do His work on Earth until His return. Look at the power of the do-good seed!

Check out your life. Examine the seeds you've been sowing through your actions. Have they been sown from a heart of love or from a motive of selfishness? Pay attention to the tests you face and look for opportunities to sow love into the lives of others through your actions.

If you haven't been reaping a good harvest, evaluate what you have been sowing. Whether in the areas of finances, relationships, or health, ask God to show you what you need to do to receive the type of harvest you desire. You may need to give more of your finances, be friendlier to others, or make an adjustment in your eating habits. God will speak to you and show you what action you should take in your particular situation.

It takes more than just *knowing* the Word to see results; you need to be a *doer* of the Word as well. You receive daily opportunities to express godly actions. Take advantage of them, knowing that when you do, a boomerang of blessings, abundance, and prosperity is headed your way!

Review Nuggets

In order to experience the abundant life God has designed for you, you must be not just a hearer of the Word, but also a doer. Your actions will set your course in life so it is important that they line up with the Word of God.

The cycle of seedtime and harvest is a spiritual law that governs life. As a boomerang returns when thrown, the seeds you sow will determine the type of harvest you receive in life—good or bad.

Actions that produce positive results are those that are based on the love of God. You will be tested by the enemy to see how you will handle challenging situations, so purpose to respond with love. Sow a do-good seed and God will demonstrate His love to you.

Foundation Scripture

Be not deceived; God is not mocked: for whatsoever a man soweth, that shall he also reap.

Galatians 6:7

Practical Application

What have you experienced in life as a result of sowing the wrong seeds? What kind of harvest would you like to reap in the future? You can change your future for the better, starting today! When opportunities arise, sow a do-good seed. Begin to write the do-good seeds you sow in your journal, and note every blessing that comes your way as a result.

Just Do It!

Several years ago, a very popular slogan ran with a very poignant message. It wasn't big band music, it wasn't an array or burst of colorful fireworks, but the message behind these three small words was so powerful and provocative that you saw them just about everywhere . . . *Just do it!* This simple statement very powerfully provokes action. You probably remember that slogan—and you may even remember it spurring you toward your goal.

Motivational speaker John Mason once said, "Don't wait for your ship to come in; swim out to meet it!" This describes the attitude of many successful people. They make up their minds to do whatever it takes to succeed. That's what we should all do—put action behind what we believe. Let me give you an illustration. Let's say God spoke to you in a dream and told you He would make all of your dreams come true if you remembered *everything* He said when you woke up. However, when morning came and your alarm sounded, you sprang out of bed and your heart sank because you realized you *didn't* remember everything God spoke to you in the dream! The promise *was* there for you to attain all your dreams, but you couldn't remember. Consequently you couldn't *act* upon it to get the results you desired.

If given the chance, you, like most people, would do whatever is necessary to receive the things that would help you realize your dreams and goals. However, more often than not, people fail to achieve their dreams. Some people know God's plan for their lives. Their faith was once stirred up by it, but they didn't act upon it, and ultimately forgot God's instruction. Because they didn't carry out God's plan, they live the same way year after year, never enjoying the benefits of what God has in store for them.

The decision to *just do it* is yours. Only you can decide to do the things that will take you to your destination and fulfill your dreams. You may have to leave your comfort zone to act on what you believe, but the result will make it well worth it. Don't get discouraged as you move forward. Doing nothing will net you nothing in the end.

You may have to leave your comfort zone to act on what
you believe, but the result will make it well worth it.

UNDERSTAND AND TAKE ACTION

In Matthew 13:23, Jesus discussed different types of soil, which signifies the spirit of a man who receives the Word of God. He said,

> But he that received seed into the good ground is he that heareth the word, and understandeth it; which also beareth fruit, and bringeth forth, some an hundredfold, some sixty, some thirty.

"Good ground" is the spirit of a man who holds on to the Word of God. He reads, understands, applies, and acts upon it. Notice that Jesus said you must *hear* and *understand* in order for the Word to produce in your life. *Understanding must precede action.*

Have you ever heard the saying, "The road to destruction is paved with good intentions"? Though it may sound harsh, it is true. Intending to take action and never actually doing it are the same thing. You may have great intentions of following the map that God has provided for you through His Word, but your good intentions alone won't lead to your God-intended destination.

For example, if you know being born again is the first step toward living a happy and fulfilled life, yet you choose not to act upon what you know, then your failure to act will cause you to miss out on your salvation. Therefore, you will never live life to the fullest and reach the expected end God has prepared for you. *Intending* to do something and actually doing it can mean the difference between seeing God's goodness manifested in your life or not. Get past the point of *good intentions* and actually *do* the Word.

GET A PLAN OF ACTION

Both you and God have active roles to play in your reaching your destination. God is not a magician, and the Bible isn't a magic book. It takes discipline, labor, and diligence—*a plan of action*—to put the Word of God to work in your life. While it is necessary to put careful thought and consideration into a plan, there comes a time when you have to put that plan into action and *just do it.*

For example, if you're trying to achieve monetary increase and freedom from debt (both are a part of the abundant living God has planned for you), you need to come up with a plan that will help you reach your goal. Start by paying off your outstanding debts. Live within your means, pay your bills on time, apply wisdom to your spending, and open a savings account so you can put money aside *every* pay period. These are only a few steps, and they should be incorporated into your plan. When these are coupled with the spiritual principles that govern finances, they will lead you into the plan God has for you.

Physical health is another area where your actions will ensure that you maintain the divine health God has promised you. Ask yourself, "What is my plan?" Don't allow yourself to be careless when it comes to your physical health. The Word of God says that your body is the *temple,* or the *dwelling place,* of His Holy Spirit (1 Corinthians 6:19). By taking the initiative to search God's Word for what He has to say about your physical health and healing, you can avoid being forced to do so out of fear in the future. The time to take authority and speak the Word of God over your physical health and well-being is *before* things begin to go wrong. Do you have a plan of action for your physical health? Are you currently practicing good eating habits? Do you exercise regularly and get enough rest? These things should be part of a consistent regimen so you can walk in total health.

If spiritual growth is your area of concern, develop a plan for growing spiritually. Purpose in your heart to attend church, regardless of how you feel. You will feel much better after feeding and cultivating your spirit, and you can look forward to additional activities after spending time in church. Set aside time to pray. Prayer will strengthen your spirit. It will help direct and guide you when you are faced with difficult decisions.

Read the Word and confess Scriptures. This will prepare you spiritually, physically, and mentally to do what God requires of you. Walk in love. Have you ever heard the adage "You can catch more flies with honey than with vinegar"? This just so happens to be true. You are much more effective in winning people's support—and winning them to Christ—when you operate in love. Choosing to walk in love, regardless of the difficult people you may encounter, will have a more positive effect than responding in the same manner they do. Rejoice in the fact that you acted in love and not revenge. This will have a significant, positive impact on those around you. Lasting impressions change opinions and lives!

> *Read the Word and confess Scriptures. This will prepare you spiritually, physically, and mentally to do what God requires of you.*

God loves you and desires for you to experience *all* that He has. He provides you with instructions that will set you on the path to your appointed destination. Your role in staying on course is to read and understand the instructions. His Word is not just another option in your life—it's the final authority! So *plan* your actions and implement them around the Word. The results will not disappoint you!

FOOLISH OR WISE? IT'S YOUR CHOICE!

The Bible says that a wise man is strong and knowledge increases his strength (Proverbs 24:5). So be wise in your decisions! If you think back over your life, can you remember anything you've done that you would consider foolish? Well, the good news is, we learn many lessons as we go through life. The key is to apply what we've learned to future actions and decisions. Be a wise person, make wise decisions, and increase in strength.

> And every one that heareth these sayings of mine, and doeth them not, shall be likened unto a foolish man. (Matthew 7:26)

The choice is pretty clear, right? You can be wise, or you can be foolish. The question is, what are you *doing* with what you hear? According to the Bible, if you are not applying the Word, you are being foolish. Take time to evaluate whether the Word has become operative in your life. Whose words do you listen to when you are stressed out and under pressure? What do you do when you are depressed, have financial problems, or need to experience healing? The issue may not be that you aren't *getting* the Word, but that you aren't *doing* anything with the Word you're getting. If you have fallen short in this area, don't give up; just decide not to let the problem continue.

The wisdom of God is synonymous with the Word of God and will produce abundance in your life. The book of Proverbs teaches that wisdom is the principal thing (Proverbs 4:7), and encourages us to honor it. Wisdom is the ability to successfully apply the knowledge you have from God's Word. It is knowing what to do in your spirit when you don't know what to do in your natural ability or mental capacity.

Knowing that the wisdom of God *is* the Word of God, you could read Proverbs 4:7, 8 like this:

> [The Word of God] is the principal thing; therefore get [the Word of God]: and with all thy getting get understanding. Exalt [the

Word of God], and [the Word of God] shall promote thee: [the Word of God] shall bring thee to honour, when thou dost embrace [the Word of God].

A wise person hears God's Word, and acts on it. This is God's program for success and discovering His will for your life. As you hear and do what He says, it will produce supernatural results. It's that simple.

A wise person hears God's Word, and acts on it.

DO WHAT YOU READ AND HEAR

When you act on the specific instructions you receive from God, the real breakthrough will manifest. When you do what you read in the Word, God will show you specific details that pertain to your life. Following His directions will bring success. He will show you how to better run your business, where to go to tap into the necessary finances, and whatever other specific directions you need to reach your destiny.

Noah is an example. God gave him specific measurements in the building of the ark. Noah wasn't a shipbuilder by any means, but when the wisdom of God was manifested, he acted on what he heard. Through this, God was able to deliver His people from a worldwide flood that destroyed every living thing, except for the life preserved on the ark. God used Noah to bring to pass His perfect will on the Earth because He knew that Noah would not hesitate to exercise the wisdom He instilled in him to accomplish this great thing (Genesis 6:18; Hebrews 11:7).

If you're seeking to fulfill the will of God for your life and want to see His promises become more in your life than a pie-in-the-sky dream, begin seeking God's Wisdom, His Word, and acting on it. No matter how much head knowledge you have, you will never escape the land of average until the wisdom of God becomes rooted in your heart to such a point that you are moved to act on it without hesitation. When you make it a priority to seek the wisdom of God and be a doer instead

of a hearer, you position yourself to live the good life and reach your
ultimate destiny!

> *When you make it a priority to seek the wisdom of God*
> *and be a doer instead of a hearer, you position yourself to*
> *live the good life and reach your ultimate destiny!*

Review Nuggets

True success is achieved only by seeking the wisdom of God and acting on it. Receiving the Word and acting on it classifies you as a wise person. When you are grounded in the Word of God, you will have the results. Implement the strategy for carrying out and applying the Word in your life.

Foundation Scripture

And every one that heareth these sayings of mine, and doeth them not, shall be likened unto a foolish man, which built his house upon the sand: And the rains descended, and the floods came, and the winds blew, and beat upon that house; and it fell: and great was the fall of it.

Matthew 7:26–27

Practical Application

Having a plan is the key to achieving success in life. Without a clear-cut plan for practically applying the Word to your everyday life, you won't see the results you want. Choose an area of your life in which you would like to see change. It may be your finances, your physical health, your relationships with others, or your spiritual growth. In your journal, write down a specific, step-by-step plan for reaching your goal.

Act on Faith

Now that you are beginning to understand God's sequence for reaching your destiny—words, thoughts, feelings, decision, actions, habits, and character—you can better position yourself to fulfill your purpose in life. Acting on the Word of God is key to achieving success. Make sure you are doing things that correspond with your faith.

Faith is a practical demonstration of your confidence in God and His Word. You can't have faith without action; the two go hand in hand. When you believe the Word of God, you have to act on it—it's just that simple. Your actions have to harmonize with your faith in order for the Word to become reality in your life.

LOCATE YOUR *SELF* BEFORE YOU ACT

Acting on the Word prematurely only leads to frustration and is often the result of false thinking and presumption rather than faith. For this reason, it is important that you locate your faith level before stepping out on something.

Finances are an area in which people often make serious blunders where their faith is concerned. Faith has both a spiritual and a practical side. Yes, I believe you should confess the Word of God out loud concerning your finances. Confessions, such as, "I'm out of debt. My needs are met. I have plenty more to put in store," will always build your faith.

However, this doesn't mean that you should govern your finances as if you have thousands of dollars in the bank when you don't.

Many times, Believers become so spiritually "deep" that they lose sight of the practical side of their faith. People declare, "I'm prosperous! I'm rich! I'm wealthy!" and then they spend beyond their means or get themselves into debt trying to maintain a façade. That's false prosperity. Remember, faith is a *practical* demonstration of your confidence in God and His Word. While you can confess that you are a millionaire, that doesn't mean you should write a check for a million dollars and try to deposit it in your bank account. Yes, you may be on your way to millionaire status, but you shouldn't buy things you can't afford in order to make a statement. That's not faith—that's foolishness.

> *Faith is a* practical *demonstration of your confidence in God and His Word.*

You may be declaring that you are wealthy even though you have only thirty thousand dollars in the bank. Now, while your *confession* is that you operate like a billionaire, in the billion-flow, your *corresponding action* is limited to the thirty thousand dollars that you have. You can't spend more than that, because it is all you have at the time. What you *can* do is ask God to tell you how much to give, so that He can multiply your seed sown and eventually bring you into financial wealth. Now *that* would be a proper corresponding action!

Keep declaring your faith, because it is through your declarations that you are exercising your faith muscles. As opportunities arise for you to step out on what you believe, perhaps through sowing a financial seed, take advantage of them. Act in accordance with what you believe, but be practical. When you do, you will begin to see increase.

Another example is in the area of your health. If you are experiencing physical challenges in your body and your doctor has prescribed medication to help the situation, don't abandon the doctor's advice and prescription and simply confess that you are healed. The Word comes first, so making faith confessions where divine health is concerned is extremely important. Declaring that you are healed will help to protect you from sickness, disease, and the attacks of the enemy against your physical body. However, don't abandon the practical side of the situation—take your medicine! God can work through natural medicine and the wisdom of a doctor to help bring your healing to pass.

> *Declaring that you are healed will help to protect you from sickness, disease, and the attacks of the enemy against your physical body.*

You may be wondering how far you can reasonably go where your corresponding actions are concerned. I'll tell you that I spent years saying, "I am a millionaire," before actually reaching millionaire status. But God honored my confession while teaching me valuable lessons about stewardship and managing my finances along the way. Millionaire status was the desire of my heart, and I surrounded myself with people of like faith who would join me in my confession of faith.

Working on the object of your faith is similar to being in a weight room developing your muscles. When you confess and act on what you believe, you are developing your faith. Every practical action you take based on the power of God's Word brings you that much closer to your goal.

You don't see immediate changes in your body when you start working out, so don't be discouraged when you don't see immediate results where your faith is concerned. Don't stop speaking and acting on what you believe! Just make sure that your actions line up with the Word of God and match your level of faith. Keep meditating on the Word until your faith rises to higher levels. Then you can step out into bigger endeavors with confidence.

WRONG ACTIONS DO NOT LINE UP

You may think that you can go pretty far in faith if you believe God and you are ready for what He wants to do in your life, and you can. But when you act out of ignorance, it will cause more harm than good. For example, if you write a check knowing the money is not in the bank, the result could mean jail time! God will not bless an illegal activity. He won't tell you to write a bad check. During a finance convention one year, someone wrote a check to me for ten thousand dollars and attached a note to it. The note said, "Don't deposit this check yet because I'm in the process of believing the Lord to put the money in the bank." That's not faith; that's foolishness!

God won't tell you to act beyond what is legal. He won't tell you to go beyond what is true in His Word or tell you to take action that doesn't correspond with your faith. Actions that don't line up with faith will only get you into trouble. So don't do anything that is out of line with God's Word. If you want to write a big check as a demonstration of your faith, thank God that one day He will bring that amount of money into your hands, and wait until He does. In the meantime, use wisdom with your finances, open a savings account, and take advantage of God's system of seedtime and harvest.

Actions that don't line up with faith will only get you into trouble.

BUILD YOUR FAITH MUSCLES

Building your faith is not hard. In fact, you can find creative ways to do it. One way to strengthen your faith is by giving yourself something visual to hold on to. A woman from our congregation decided she had had enough of struggling to make ends meet. She was fed up with having to pay a car note, a mortgage, and other monthly obligations. It seemed as if she had "too much week" left over between pay periods. So she decided to do something creative to jump-start her faith for financial increase.

One way to strengthen your faith is by giving yourself something visual to hold on to.

This woman bought a large poster board, drew several mountains on it, and labeled each one with the name of a debt. Every day, several times a day, she would call out the names of her creditors and the amounts she owed each one. She would end her confession time by praising and thanking God for her debt deliverance *before* she saw anything happen. It wasn't long before every single mountain of debt on that board had been paid in full! She is now debt-free and works because she wants to, not because she has to.

My wife, Taffi, and I did something similar. When we were in debt and struggling to make ends meet every month, we gathered our bills together. We wrote the date and our declaration of independence from debt on a sheet of paper. When we began this process, we experienced demonic attacks, but we used that piece of paper as a point of contact for God's power to intervene on our behalf. Each time we prayed, we placed our hands on our bag of bills, bearing the words "debt-free," and made our confessions based on God's Word. Under the words "debt-free," we listed the things we were expecting to have that would help us out of our situation: favor, unexpected income, and supernatural debt-release. Our prayers for miraculous debt cancellation were answered. It took time, but we no longer live the way we did. Today, God is fulfilling His plan for our lives—debt-free!

The Bible brings up this point in James 2:14: "What doth it profit, my brethren, though a man say he hath faith, and have not works? can faith save him?" It goes on to ask: if someone needed food and clothes, would you just send the person away with a verbal blessing? Who does it help, if nothing is done to address the immediate need? Verse 17 says, "Even so faith, if it hath not works, is dead, being alone." You must take action with the faith you have in your heart.

You must take action with the faith you have in your heart.

DEAD FAITH WALKING

I want to emphasize that there are many people who try to operate on a higher level of faith than they have developed. This is no different from a guy trying to bench-press more weight than he knows he has the strength to lift. He *knows* he can press only 120 pounds. Yet because he sees everybody else in the gym lifting 300 pounds or more, his emotions get riled up, and he tries to do something he's not prepared to do. As a result, he ends up hurting himself.

The same thing happens spiritually among Christians. We can get so excited about what's being preached in church that we overlook the fact that we've not yet developed our faith to the necessary level. It takes time, diligence, and consistency to develop your spirit's capacity to receive greater things from God. Believers want to "name it and claim it," but often they aren't willing to put in the effort necessary to build their faith.

It takes time, diligence, and consistency to develop your spirit's capacity to receive greater things from God.

We've got to be careful to not allow our emotions to move us to do something that is really more fantasy-based than faith-based. That's like dead faith walking. Even though you may be *doing* something, it's not really based on faith. Ask yourself, "All right, where am I right now in my faith? I didn't have enough faith last week. I think I'd better exercise my faith muscles some more." The Bible talks about *walking by faith,* so go ahead and start walking your faith out, one day at a time.

Another example of "dead faith walking" is acting out according to someone else's faith. Most of the time, this will not produce results. If you know someone who gave her car away and received another one debt-free within a month, that isn't a sign for you to do the same! You may just end up stuck without transportation. You have to have faith in the Word of God for yourself, based on your own personal meditation time and experience with Him.

What many people call "faith" isn't faith at all. It is just high expectation based on the wrong information, like expecting to receive a car debt-free based on information that came from your friend. Don't ever do something simply because you saw another person do it. Find out what that person did to get their faith to that point, and then dig into the Scriptures for yourself until they become real to *you*. Then when God speaks something specific to your heart, you will have confidence that your actions will produce results.

Faith should always be based on the Word of God. If something doesn't line up with the Bible, you have no foundation upon which to build your faith. Your ideas or personal desires are not guaranteed. The only thing that is guaranteed is the Word.

The only thing that is guaranteed is the Word.

If you believe that God has spoken to your heart about something, search the Scriptures. Does it line up with the way God operates? Do you have a Scripture on which to stand? Do you have peace from the Holy Spirit about it, or do you have unrest? These are all key questions to consider before you take action.

DON'T GIVE UP

If you discover that you've overextended yourself or made mistakes where your faith actions are concerned, don't get discouraged. Most of all, don't give up, cave in, and quit. For example, if you bought a car that you knew you couldn't afford, but at the time you really believed it was a faith move, don't panic. Acknowledge to yourself and God that you made a mistake, return the vehicle to the dealer, and buy something that is in your price range instead. Don't go deeper into debt trying to prove something, but don't give up the dream of owning that car one day, either. Purpose in your heart to accomplish your goal by trusting and believing God and acting wisely.

Achieving your destiny requires bold, courageous faith. When the Word of God is planted firmly in your heart, you will have what you need. In addition, the more you meditate on God's Word, the more confident you will become in your decisions *and* the more your discernment will kick in when you are about to act foolishly. The more you demonstrate your confidence in God and His Word, the closer you will be to achieving the good life. Make sure your actions are Bible-based, and let them steer you in the right direction. That's real faith!

Review Nuggets

Real Bible faith is the practical expression of your confidence in God and His Word. Meditate on the Word until your heart is firmly established in it. Don't act based on fantasy or presumption; God will not bless that. Combine the spiritual and practical aspects of faith so that you will achieve the results you truly want. When you are acting in faith, your behavior will line up with the Word and the witness of the Holy Spirit.

Foundation Scripture

Now the just shall live by faith: but if any man draw back, my soul shall have no pleasure in him.

Hebrews 10:38

Practical Application

Sometimes what we call "faith" is really high expectation based on the wrong information. Make sure your information is based on the Word of God. Make a list of the top five things you would like to see come to pass in your life. Write them down in your journal. On another page, make a list of the practical things you can do to accomplish those goals, and on the other side of the page, write down the corresponding spiritual things you can do to achieve your destiny.

Step 6

Establish Healthy Habits

Habits: How They Are Formed

Who you are today is a result of the choices you made yesterday. Your character is a direct result of the habits you have formed in life. A professional athlete is highly skilled in his field because of the habits formed through daily practice. Likewise, you will develop in areas that ultimately affect who you are and who you will become *based on your habits.* The Merriam-Webster Dictionary defines a *habit* as "a settled tendency or usual manner of behavior, or a behavior pattern acquired by frequent repetition."

> *Your character is a direct result of the habits you have formed in life.*

When was the last time you took a good look at who you are? I'm talking about conducting a self-inventory to evaluate who you are based on your habits. The things you do regularly—every day—contribute greatly to shaping your identity. In *The Writings of Benjamin Franklin,* Benjamin Franklin wrote, "I believe long habits of virtue have a sensible effect on the countenance." That is a very accurate statement. When you form positive habits that align with respect for and understanding of who God is and what His Word says, your very countenance will reflect that. Your habits shape and form your character, and your character is you!

Experts say it takes twenty-one days to make or break a habit. Health and fitness gurus recommend sticking with a good exercise regimen for at least twenty-one days to allow healthy practices to become habits. Many of us relate to having bad habits where food and exercise are concerned. If you form a habit of eating fast food every day, you compromise good health as a result. Your identity will conform more and more to that particular habit. Having no discipline with food causes you to develop character that is marked by lasciviousness, or lack of restraint. If you struggle with bad eating habits, that can carry over into your finances and other areas as well.

On the flip side, if you develop the habits of eating a healthy breakfast every morning, drinking lots of water every day, and making sure that you exercise three to four days out of the week, you will become disciplined, reaping the benefits of divine health. The habits you form have the potential to either help or hinder you in your spiritual walk, and your decisions directly affect the habits you develop.

EXAMINE YOUR HABITS

Everything starts with a decision. Actions precede the habits that are formed in your life, and your decisions are the basis for your actions. I believe habits ultimately begin with the decisions you make based on either the Word of God or an outside source. The moment you make a choice to do something, you are on your way to forming a habit. The problem is, if your decisions oppose the Bible, you will soon find that you have bad habits that are hard to break.

For example, choosing to listen to ungodly music every day and keeping your radio programmed to secular stations will eventually cause you to develop a habit of listening to that kind of music. The words you hear will penetrate your spirit and affect your mindset. Eventually, your whole life will reflect what you have been feeding your spirit. This is how habits are formed—by making simple, everyday decisions.

Every day you are faced with choices that have the potential to build habits. People who are slaves to addictive behaviors didn't become that way overnight. They developed their addictions based on repeated decisions. Someone who is hooked on pornography, for example, had to start somewhere. That person's decision to watch an X-rated movie or log on to an Internet porn site fed a desire that became difficult to turn off once it was turned on. The same is true for someone who smokes or does drugs. That first decision to "try it" activated a habit. Habits such as lying, flying off the handle when you are upset, or fornicating all start with the same seemingly small decisions.

God's Word must be the final authority in your life. Let the Word of God determine your thinking. Then everything else will spring from a godly mindset.

Take time to examine your habits. Would you say that you have good or bad habits? Do they line up with God's Word, which is His will for your life? If you have habits and desires that are born out of sinful compulsions, you are on a sure path to spiritual ruin and will miss what God has planned for your life.

Even the apostle Paul had to battle certain compulsions in life. He wrote about it in Romans 7:19: "For I fail to practice the good deeds I desire to do, but the evil deeds that I do not desire to do are what I am [ever] doing" (AMP). Paul went on to explain his struggle to do what he desired to do instead of the things he did not desire to do. He examined the battle between the carnal and the spiritual aspects of man. "Now if I do what I do not desire to do, it is no longer I doing it [It is not myself that acts], but the sin [principle] which dwells within me [fixed and operating in my soul]" (Romans 7:20, AMP). This is key to understanding how to deal with bad habits: You have to submit to the Word of God in order to break them.

> *This is key to understanding how to deal with bad habits: You have to submit to the Word of God in order to break them.*

Often, though we try to do what is right, it is a struggle because of the way we operated before we were born again. Creating bad habits by consistently making the wrong choices will only make it that much harder to overcome that old nature. It is vital that you allow your decisions to be governed by God's Word and not by your emotions.

There may be a habit that you have been wrestling with for years. It could stem from a way of thinking that has been established in your mind for a long time. Perhaps it is a mindset you adopted growing up, or maybe you were influenced by a close friend or relative. If your thinking does not line up with the Word of God, you will end up deciding to do things that will create bad habits. Unfortunately for many people, by the time they realize they need to change, they've created habits that have serious consequences. You don't want to put yourself in that position.

GODLY EXAMPLES

1. David.

There are many wonderful examples of great men and women of God who developed good habits that led them to God's destination for their lives. Some of them, like David, developed a habit of praying and praising God. Because of David's lifestyle of prayer and praise, God consistently rescued David from trouble during tough times.

2. The Proverbs 31 woman.

To this day, we don't know who the woman mentioned in Proverbs 31 was, but we do know that she exhibited godly character born out of godly habits. We know for sure that she was a woman who was determined to do the right thing at all times. It appears her determination to do the right thing kept her from destructive habits.

Proverbs 31:13–15 says, "She seeks out wool and flax and works with willing hands [to develop it]. She is like the merchant ships loaded with foodstuffs; she brings her household's food from a far [country]. She rises while it is yet night and gets [spiritual] food for her household and assigns her maids their tasks" (AMP). This woman was in the habit of getting up early to take care of her household. She was a hard worker. As a result, she was "loaded"! She was pleasing in God's sight because she did what was right. Her habits took her to God's destination for her life.

3. Daniel.

Daniel is another example of someone with good habits. He was a man who always walked in the blessings of God. He was determined to be faithful to the Lord. He maintained good eating habits, a consistent prayer life, and an attitude of excellence and integrity.

When he was invited to eat of the meat the king offered him, he refused. "Daniel was determined not to defile himself by eating the food and wine given to them by the king. He asked the chief of staff for permission not to eat these unacceptable foods" (Daniel 1:8, NLT). At that time, disobeying the king's order was an offense punishable by death. However, Daniel was so diligent in his quest to stick with his diet of vegetables and water that he was willing to take that risk. His mind was made up. He refused to eat the rich foods offered by the king. God's blessing was on his life, and in whatever obstacle or challenge he encountered, he came out on top.

God even worked on Daniel's behalf by softening others' hearts toward him. The Bible says, "Now God made Daniel to find favor, compassion, and loving-kindness with the chief of the eunuchs" (Daniel 1:9, AMP). Daniel's spiritual and natural habits found him favor in the eyes of God and man.

IDENTIFY YOUR WEAK POINTS

In order to defeat bad habits, you need to identify your weak points. In what areas are you most susceptible to temptation? It could be a particular eating habit you have, or something as extreme as looking at pornography on the Internet. Regardless of the area, identify where you have a particular weakness and ask God to help you.

I am fairly strict where my eating and exercise habits are concerned. While my body may scream for apple pie, I know there is something bigger at stake—my health. Though I may splurge every now and then, I don't consume as much sugar as I used to.

Another bad habit I have overcome is anger. I used to have a habit of completely flying off the handle when I got upset about something.

I would get so angry that I would even cuss people out who were trying to help me! The Lord told me that if I didn't get control over my temper, I would end up in a casket way before my time. I realized I had to change.

Identify your weakest point. Is it food? Premarital sex? Anger? Lying? Being honest with yourself is the only way to start the process. When you deal with lasciviousness head-on, the results of bad habits will stop.

SELFISHNESS: THE ROOT OF BAD HABITS

Bad habits are rooted in selfishness. That habit you enjoy so much, that you know is bad for you, is satisfying to your flesh. Even though you know it is wrong, there is no denying that it feels good. Getting back at someone who has hurt or wronged you *feels* good. Overeating or eating sweets all the time *feels* good. Having sex outside of marriage *feels* good. But in the end, it will destroy you.

To identify whether you are living a selfish life, let's take a look at what it means to be selfish. The Merriam-Webster Dictionary defines *selfish* as being "concerned excessively or exclusively with oneself . . . without regard for others." That's what bad habits are all about—you, and how you feel at the time. And when you are involved in a bad habit, you are most likely having a negative impact on others.

If you had a conversation with someone about a particular bad habit that he can't seem to break, you may hear him say something like, "I don't know why the devil keeps making me do this!" This statement may provide an excuse to continue the wrong behavior, but it is far from the truth. The devil can't *make* anybody do anything he or she doesn't want to do. All he can do is make suggestions and plant thoughts to get you to think a certain way. When you act on those thoughts, a habit begins to form. Satan specializes in addiction, so any word he can get you to act on has the potential to become a bad habit that will hurt you.

On the other hand, God wants to bless you. His words will set in motion a pattern of blessings that will cause you to live the abundant life. When you make up your mind to get in line with His Word and His

way of doing things, you will experience all that He has preordained
for your life. By walking in love rather than selfishness, and desiring to
please God more than yourself or others, you will discover that you *can*
break out of the addictive cycle of bad habits.

God wants to bless you.

The worst thing to do when you want to break a bad habit is to try to
do it in your own ability. This will fail every time and leave you frustrated. God's method of getting you out of addictive behavior involves
a process of employing His sequence of words, thoughts, emotions,
decisions, and actions.

The Bible contains everything you need to stop craving cigarettes or
overeating or to break any other bad habit you may struggle with. The
Scriptures are the key to your breakthrough, so get in the Word! The
rewards far outweigh the temporary challenges you will encounter on
your way to freedom.

DEAL WITH BAD HABITS

When you begin to tackle the mental strongholds that have kept you in
a destructive cycle of bad habits, you will realize you have to fight for
your breakthrough.

For example, if you are tempted to commit adultery, which could
easily turn into an addictive habit and life pattern, trace your thought
pattern. Have you chosen to watch pornography or hang out with people who are sexually promiscuous? Those choices will influence your
decisions, and those decisions will lead to the actions that form habits.

Friends, music, magazines, romance novels, and movies can all create an environment that makes it nearly impossible for you to resist
temptation and break bad habits. Satan knows how to get your mind
going in a particular direction. You have to defer to what I call the
replacement principle, meaning you must replace negative thoughts
with the Word of God. Remember, it is not enough to remove sinful

thoughts. You must *replace* them with thoughts and desires from the Word. God doesn't leave you to fix the bad stuff yourself. Do what is right, and He will fix what is wrong. Get into the Word, and you will be equipped to triumph over bad habits.

Putting the replacement principle to work in your life basically involves two steps. The first step is to *stop doing the things that get you into trouble.* If you are a compulsive shopper, stop window shopping. If you are not disciplined in this area, you may want to limit shopping visits to times when you need specific items, and then only purchase those items. Another idea would be to have a friend or relative who is disciplined in this area shop with you, and make yourself accountable to him or her for your spending. If surfing the Internet for pornography is an issue for you, put a blocker on your computer, fast from using the computer at all, or have the Internet taken off your computer. Do whatever you need to do to overcome these bad habits.

The second step is to *replace negative thoughts with positive ones from God's Word.* The Bible says, "Finally, brethren, whatsoever things are true, whatsoever things are honest, whatsoever things are just, whatsoever things are pure, whatsoever things are lovely, whatsoever things are of good report; if there be any virtue, and if there be any praise, think on these things" (Philippians 4:8). What you think about will determine what type of habits you have, and ultimately what type of person you become.

You can break bad habits by applying the Word of God. Psalm 119:9 says, "Wherewithal shall a young man cleanse his way? by taking heed thereto according to thy word." Build a solid future by developing the right habits today. Whether or not you arrive at your destination will depend on it!

BREAK THE UNBREAKABLE

Every person has faced habits that seemed unbreakable. However, for the Christian, there is victory over every bad habit. They don't have to rule your life. The Word of God and the help of the Holy Spirit are your keys to breaking bad habits forever. While it takes effort on your part, with God's help you can break free from the habits and behaviors that are hindering your destiny.

> *The Word of God and the help of the Holy Spirit*
> *are your keys to breaking bad habits forever.*

If you find yourself in a downward spiral of bad habits, it's time to break out and make a change by applying the principles of the Word and employing the Holy Spirit. First, you must acknowledge there are certain bad habits you have embraced. Second, you must recognize that if you don't change, your growth will stop and your future will be negatively impacted. Finally, you must invite God to help you get out of your situation.

The Holy Spirit is a gentleman. He will never force you to do things His way. He will try to guide you gently down the right path, often using what I like to call "spiritual bumpers" to help get you back on track. Ultimately, His effectiveness in helping you break bad habits depends on your willingness to yield to Him when He leads you. Whenever you do something or are *about* to do something that feeds your bad habit, a sense of conviction will rise within your spirit. This is the Holy Spirit's way of getting your attention and letting you know to *stop!* When you ignore His promptings, you make it much harder to break a habit.

For example, if you have gotten into the habit of engaging in premarital sex, you have set yourself on a destructive path. You can change your behavior by recognizing that fornication is wrong and applying the Word of God to your life. As you renew your mind in this area, embrace God's plan for sex within the context of marriage. Ask the Holy Spirit to help you, and He will begin to disrupt your sinful patterns. He will increase that feeling of conviction when you are about to do something that is not in line with His Word. It's up to you to submit to what He is doing in your life.

When the Word is firmly established in your spirit, it will be the first thing you think of when you are faced with tempting situations. Like a buffer against the attacks of the enemy, the Word will shield you from the devil's attempts to keep you locked in the vicious cycle of bad habits.

I can't emphasize enough the power of words. Create the habits you want by speaking them into existence. Come up with your own confessions based on God's Word and say them every day. Don't let a day go by without confessing that you are free and delivered from whatever you are struggling with. Your mouth sets your course in life, so your words are pivotal in breaking bad habits. Don't let a day go by without confessing that you are free and delivered from whatever you are struggling with.

> *Don't let a day go by without confessing that you are free and delivered from whatever you are struggling with.*

Overcoming lascivious habits is a matter of making sure your spirit is in control at all times. Now you can see why it is so critical that you don't neglect your time spent in the Word. Spend time in God's presence, and surround yourself with people who are working on maintaining their deliverance as well. Constantly filling yourself with the Word of God is the key to freedom and success.

Review Nuggets

The words you receive and the choices you make as a result of your mindset will cause certain habits to form. Your habits play a significant role in the type of character you develop, and ultimately the destination that you reach in life. For this reason, it is critical that you make decisions that are in line with God's Word. When you are faced with a choice, evaluate whether the action you take will contribute to a potentially disastrous habit.

If you have allowed the wrong mindset to shape your decisions, begin to renew your mind with God's Word. This is the key to breaking bad habits. Turn to God by making the Word of God your final authority. When you ask Him to help you get out of an addictive cycle of bad habits, He will. It is then up to you to yield to His direction when He attempts to lead you out.

When the devil brings suggestions to your mind, cast them down by speaking the Word of God. Replace wrong thoughts by meditating on God's Word. This will, in turn, affect the feelings, decisions, and actions that lead to habits. Don't try to break bad habits through your own ability. Instead, rely on God, the strength of Jesus, and the wisdom of the Holy Spirit to help you overcome your challenges.

Foundation Scripture

Casting down imaginations, and every high thing that exalteth itself against the knowledge of God, and bringing into captivity every thought to the obedience of Christ.

2 Corinthians 10:5

Practical Application

In your journal, write down any habits you feel are holding you back and hindering your spiritual growth. Then write down steps you will take, using God's Word, to change. Keep track of your progress on a daily basis and write down your victories as they come.

The Power of
Discipline

Discipline is a powerful, yet often neglected, aspect of Christianity. I've discovered that many Christians love to shout, claim their blessings, and go through emotional displays of excitement about God's promises, but aren't willing to *do* what is necessary to get the results they want. *Discipline* has become a dirty word in the Body of Christ, and because of this, Believers are not seeing the manifestation of their dreams. The problem isn't God or the devil. The real dilemma lies in a lack of self-discipline.

Discipline, in the Merriam-Webster Dictionary, is defined as "training that corrects, molds, or perfects mental faculties or moral character." It is the foundation for your success, and without it you won't get very far. Reaching your destiny requires becoming disciplined in the things of God and developing the right habits. This takes commitment and a consistent, concerted effort on your part.

Discipline sets things in motion. As an example, when you are disciplined to watch your eating habits and work out at the gym every day, you are setting yourself up for success. I've noticed a change in my own life because of my decision to discipline myself in the area of my health. While I may feel the effects of a tough weight-training session the next day, the results are worth it. I'm still working on some things, but I'm glad that I've developed this habit now. I'm setting myself up for a long, strong life.

The same is true with spiritual matters. You have to discipline yourself in the things of God. Setting aside time every day for praise, prayer, and fellowship with God is a spiritual discipline you can't afford to neglect. These things are essential for your development and success.

FOLLOW JESUS' EXAMPLE

Jesus is the model for the disciplined life. We are His *disciples* on Earth, and we need to examine what that actually means. A disciple is a follower of Christ, someone who is learning His way of doing things. How can we call ourselves disciples of the Lord Jesus Christ if we don't do what He did? While Jesus is God, He was also a man who had to do the practical day-to-day things necessary to be successful in His ministry. His habits created a core foundation from which He was able to do powerful works. Let's examine four areas in which Jesus exercised discipline:

1. Jesus was disciplined in His prayer life.

Jesus had constant contact with the Father. He achieved this through the discipline of prayer. The Gospels point to Jesus' regular habit of praying alone, early in the morning. Mark 1:35 describes Jesus' prayer life: "And in the morning, rising up a great while before day, he went out, and departed into a solitary place, and there prayed." Mark 6:46 also says, "And when he had sent them away, he departed into a mountain to pray."

Jesus prayed regularly, which was evident in His ministry. He took the time to receive the Father's instructions and impartation for the day so people's lives would be changed. Everything He did, from the words He spoke to the miracles He performed, was activated by the power of prayer. So, likewise, you must make prayer a part of your day, every day. That's discipline!

2. Jesus was disciplined in His thought life and emotions.

Jesus never let His emotions get out of control. He never yielded to Satan's suggestions because He was disciplined in His thoughts and feelings. He practiced the love of God and had a mindset that was aligned with the Father's. The reason these two areas require discipline is because they can easily get out of control. They are also the two key areas Satan will *always* attack. Disciplining your mind and emotions is achieved when you choose to respond to negative situations with the Word of God.

Jesus never let His emotions get out of control.

A disciplined person sets his mind and will to counteract every ungodly thought with God's Word, with no exceptions. You must practice casting down ungodly thoughts whenever the opportunity arises. It takes discipline to reject a thought or suggestion that may feel good to your flesh. Take extra measures to memorize Scriptures so you will have the ammunition to cast down ungodly thoughts.

Practice responding correctly when you are tempted to make an emotional decision that could lead you away from the will of God for your life. Discipline yourself not to allow your life to be emotionally led. Make the Word of God your final authority, and do what it says in every situation.

Jesus was in agony in the Garden of Gethsemane, yet even then, He disciplined His emotions. I can't even begin to imagine the depths of turmoil and pressure Jesus experienced during those final hours before His crucifixion. The Word says He was depressed and deeply disturbed; He was emotional! Even still, Jesus demonstrated absolute mastery over His emotions when He said, "Father, if thou be willing, remove this cup from me: nevertheless not my will, but thine, be done" (Luke 22:42).

Jesus trained Himself to be so disciplined in the areas of thoughts and emotions that when He was faced with death and the option to avoid it, He chose to deny His emotions so He could fulfill His reason for coming to Earth. He didn't even allow the horror of the cross to move Him away from the will of God for His life.

3. *Jesus was disciplined in studying and meditating on the Word.*

We know Jesus *was* the Word of God in the flesh. However, He was also a man. Jesus had to study and meditate on the Word, just as you and I do. It was evident that He was disciplined in His study and meditation of the Scriptures because He was *always* ready to give people the biblical answers they were looking for. The Word was such a part of Him that when He spoke, things immediately happened. This type of power isn't possible without discipline.

Psalm 119:97–100 describes the power of disciplining yourself in the Word. It says:

Oh, how love I Your law! It is my meditation all the day. You, through Your commandments, make me wiser than my enemies, for [Your words] are ever before me. I have better understanding and deeper insight than all my teachers, because Your testimonies are my meditation. I understand more than the aged, because I keep Your precepts [hearing, receiving, loving, and obeying them].(AMP)

I believe this passage is a reflection of Jesus and His commitment to meditate on and be a student of the Word. He began seeking knowledge and understanding as a young boy. In fact, His discipline and diligence in the Word of God could be seen at an early age.

Luke 2:46, 47 says:

And it came to pass, that after three days they found him in the temple, sitting in the midst of the doctors, both hearing them, and asking them questions. And all that heard him were astonished at his understanding and answers.

No doubt Jesus' discipline and hunger for the things of God and the truths of the Scriptures continued throughout His teenage years and into adulthood. This obviously had everything to do with the level of power He walked in as a grown man.

4. Jesus was disciplined in His speech.

Jesus had complete control over His mouth. He even said that He spoke only what He heard from the Father (John 12:50). Can you imagine speaking *only* what your heavenly Father says to you and nothing else? You would live a truly powerful life because whatever God says is guaranteed to get results.

When Jesus' critics publicly challenged Him, He always answered them with the Word of God. He never got into strife with anyone, even though He could have, and I'm sure His flesh was tempted. Even while going through His arrest prior to the crucifixion, He could have summoned legions of angels to rescue Him and instantly destroy His enemies (Matthew 26:53), but instead, He allowed Himself to be captured. Jesus knew the power of words and was disciplined in His speech.

Every Believer would do well to follow Jesus' example in these four areas. I guarantee that if you commit to disciplining yourself in prayer, your thought life, your study and meditation of the Word, and your speech, you will begin to see negative situations and circumstances turn around. You will also position yourself for the success that you have always dreamed of.

DESIRE DISCIPLINE IN YOUR LIFE

Brian Tracy, a respected leader in the world of personal and business success, said, "People create their own success by learning what they need to learn, and then by practicing it, they become proficient at it." Nothing just happens. There is a process that you must go through in order to reach your destiny. It takes work! Your dreams won't come to pass without discipline.

I encourage you to do some research about your favorite professional athlete or musical artist. Regardless of the field, talent won't reach its full potential unless the individual is disciplined in the practice of his craft. Whether it is singing, dancing, acting, or playing sports, it takes discipline to be successful.

Let's look at it from a spiritual perspective. While God may have put the desire to do a particular thing in your heart, and you may have a knack for doing that thing exceptionally well, you need to be disciplined in that area. Discipline is the key that unlocks the desire of your heart. In order to see manifestation, you must not only desire it, but there must be discipline.

> *Discipline is the key that unlocks the desire of your heart.*

I also like to look at discipline in the sense of doing a series of drills, similar to the way a soldier trains for military service. George Washington said, "Discipline is the soul of an army. It makes small numbers formidable, procures success to the weak, and esteem to all." In fact, the Bible likens the Christian to a soldier (2 Timothy 2:3, 4). Being disciplined in the Word of God means putting yourself through intense training on a daily basis. When your life is governed by the Word, you make a point to train yourself in it. That means disciplining yourself to get up in the morning to pray like Jesus did, restraining your flesh when you want to say or do something that opposes God's Word, and allowing the Word to transform your thinking through scheduled meditation time.

The reason the Bible doesn't work for some people is because it requires them to *work*, and laboring in the Word, especially when it seems as if nothing is happening, is something those people just aren't willing to do. We live in a microwave society that is always looking for a quick and easy way to success, but God honors you when you go through the right process.

It takes discipline to turn off the television and open your Bible for some quality study and meditation time, especially when you are tired and have had a long day at work. Discipline has to kick in when God wakes you up at three o'clock in the morning to pray! Having the desire is not enough. Coming to church, hearing a sermon, and taking notes are just the beginning. The real work begins when you are at home, on the job, and in situations that are uncomfortable for you. Don't give up! It is the one who remains disciplined who will reach his destiny and experience prosperity.

THE ANOINTING OF DISCIPLINE

As we've seen, the anointing is the burden-removing, yoke-destroying power of God. It is an empowerment from God to get results in every area of your life. When the anointing operates through discipline, it removes burdens and destroys yokes in your life. Discipline to do what Jesus did will set a force in motion that will propel you to biblical success.

Being disciplined means denying your flesh what it wants in order to reap the benefits of sowing to your spirit. This is probably the hardest area for Believers to master. Galatians 6:8 says, "For he that soweth to his flesh shall of the flesh reap corruption; but he that soweth to the Spirit shall of the Spirit reap life everlasting." This means that if you keep doing things to please your flesh, you will reap a negative result. If you stay in bed when you know you need to get up and pray, you'll miss something God wants to do for you or through you. You'll harvest the negative results that people harvest when they don't pray.

If you keep ignoring the Word by watching television, talking on the phone, or doing any number of other things when you could be devoting that time to God, you'll reap consequences you don't want. The Bible teaches us that if we sow to our spirit, we will reap *zoe*, which means life everlasting (*Strong's Concordance, Greek Lexicon*). It is the God-kind of life, the abundant life.

As you move into a lifestyle of discipline, there will be times when you feel like giving up, particularly when you don't see results right away, but remember not to get weary in well-doing. Every time you do something to advance your spiritual growth, you are positioning yourself for increase. Don't worry about what it looks like; continue being disciplined in the things of God. The Bible promises a rich reward.

START TODAY

Make a decision today to become disciplined in every area of your life, so that you can develop the right habits. Then you will be able to receive the power that God has made available to you in His Word. Start with things like your eating, exercise habits, and speech. Examine the areas in which you can become more disciplined, and create a plan to achieve your goals. It may require giving up your television or phone time to spend time in the Word, or making a point to get up *every* morning to pray, even if it is only for a short time.

The key is to identify areas in which you can develop discipline and begin *now*. Once you make a quality decision, all of Heaven will back you up. The Holy Spirit is standing by to help you get to the place God has designed for your life, so don't neglect your part. Become that good soldier and begin training yourself in spiritual *and* natural disciplines. As you develop a lifestyle of discipline, you will be one more step closer to reaching your destiny!

Review Nuggets

Discipline in both the natural and spiritual aspects of your life will create habits that lead to prosperity. Discipline is similar to strict training in which you deny your flesh what it wants, and instead allow your spirit to take a higher position. Disciplining yourself in the areas of prayer, thought life, study of and meditation on God's Word, and speech will position you for success. Discipline is the key to releasing the power of God in your life.

Foundation Scripture

For he that soweth to his flesh shall of the flesh reap corruption; but he that soweth to the Spirit shall of the Spirit reap life everlasting.

Galatians 6:8

Practical Application

Everyone has areas in which he or she can become more disciplined. Your habits are formed by what you are disciplined in doing, and the habits you embrace play a huge role in your success or failure in life. In your journal, identify an area in which you want to become more disciplined. Then write down three practical steps you can take to become more disciplined, and three spiritual steps as well. Now, write out a contract for this commitment and sign it.

Step 7

Develop Godly Character

Make Your Way Prosperous

Have you ever paid for something at a restaurant or convenience store and been given too much change? What would you do if you found a bag full of money and you weren't sure to whom it belonged? Many people would be tempted to keep the money and spend it on themselves. I've actually seen people thank God for money that came into their hands as a result of someone else's mistake, such as a cashier's or bank teller's oversight.

Now, I know many of us would gladly give the change back to the cashier or do what we could to find the rightful owner of the bag of money, but what if you were really struggling to make ends meet? Would doing the right thing be so easy then? God is watching to see how you handle situations like these.

Jesus says we should have life in abundance, to the full, until it overflows (John 10:10, AMP). Are you doing what you need to do to live the life God planned for you to live? Good character is an essential part of the good life. Studying and applying the Word of God will produce the thinking, emotions, decisions, actions, habits, and ultimately character, that lead to your destiny.

As you've already learned, your habits will lead you either toward or away from the good life God wants to give you. If you consistently do the wrong things, you will create habits that will take you down the wrong path. Before long, you will find yourself depressed and disappointed in life.

Conversely, if you allow your words, thoughts, emotions, decisions, actions, and habits to be governed by the Word, your character will follow suit, and you'll be very pleased with your future. If you don't like where you are right now, examine your life through the sequence of the eight steps. You can trace your character all the way back to the negative words you listened to and spoke. They produced the results you have now.

Character is critical to your success in life. You won't go very far with bad character. It will hinder what God wants to do in your life and will ultimately destroy you. Character is the most important part of this sequence, because it absolutely determines how much of God's goodness will be released into your life.

Character is doing what is right because it is right, and doing it right. It is who you are when no one is looking. I've often said that charm is who you are at the moment, but character is who you are all the time. It is based on who you've been hanging around, what habits you have developed, and the words you've allowed into your heart. Those words have framed the way you now think about yourself and the world around you. Your answer to the question I posed at the beginning of this chapter reveals a lot about your character. Strong character motivates you to do what is right, no matter what the circumstances might be.

> *Charm is who you are at the moment, but*
> *character is who you are all the time.*

The goal for every Christian is to have the character of Jesus. It is His character that allows us to be free from the stress of this world. When you refuse to develop the love of God, which is the character of Jesus, you develop the world's character instead, which is defined by the works of the flesh.

Galatians 5:19–26 describes the pitfalls of having poor character:

It is obvious what kind of life develops out of trying to get your own way all the time: repetitive, loveless, cheap sex; a stinking accumulation of mental and emotional garbage; frenzied and joy-less grabs for happiness; . . . loneliness; cutthroat competition; . . . a brutal temper; an impotence to love or be loved; divided homes and divided lives; . . . uncontrollable addictions; . . . I could go on. (The Message)

As these Scriptures outline, poor character leads to a lonely, empty life. It's born out of demanding your own way all the time. Although God wants to give you the desires of your heart, it shouldn't be at the expense of other people. You should be looking for opportunities to help somebody else. That's what God's love is all about. He gave His only Son so you and I could be free from the snare of sin and eternal death.

DO WHAT'S RIGHT BECAUSE IT'S RIGHT

The other day I received a call from a minister I know. He had been going through a rough time, and the bank was about to foreclose on his home. Just listening to this man, I could tell that his hope was broken. It was then that the Lord told me to help him keep his home.

Now, I could have decided not to follow God's instructions and to judge the man, but that would not have been the character that God has developed in me. Yes, the man made a mistake, but we've all made mistakes at one time or another. It's not my place, or anyone else's, to judge someone's shortcomings. Instead, we should look for ways to be a blessing to people, especially when they really need help. At that moment, he needed assistance, and under the direction of the Holy Spirit, I helped him with his need.

When you consciously set out to be a blessing to others in every situation you face, that's character. Do you remember the saying, "Do unto others as you would have them do unto you?" (see Matthew 7:12). Today, that adage isn't always recognized as an admirable quality, but God admires it. In fact, He will bless you if you choose to demonstrate caring for others as part of your character.

Having good character means not taking a twenty-minute break at work when you know you're only allowed fifteen minutes. It means that when the cashier at the drive-thru window gives you too much change for the meal you ordered, you give the money back. Character is looking for ways you can *give* the advantage to people rather than *take* the advantage.

> *Character is looking for ways you can* give *the advantage to people rather than* take *the advantage.*

Many people think, *Why would I want to do something like that? I mean, people are ripping me off all the time.* But when you have character, you look for ways to benefit other people. Prospering others instead of taking from them sets you up for God to do something extra special in your life.

For example, when you visit a hotel, do you feel as though you've earned the right to take some of the complementary items that help make your stay more comfortable? Do you say, "They've got enough of my money, I'm taking the toothbrush, soap, and everything I can." Well, you're not operating in character, because what you're doing won't prosper that hotel.

I remember one time I needed to take a hanger from my hotel room. I had such conviction about prospering people that I called down to the front desk and said, "Before I check out, I just want to let you know that I'm taking one of your hangers, but I'm leaving fifty dollars in an envelope to replace it."

The lady on the phone was so quiet you could have heard a pin drop. I think she was shocked by my integrity! I knew that hanger didn't cost fifty dollars, but I felt like I should leave enough to not only replace the hanger, but maybe buy a few more. It's just not right for me to do the minimum to prosper someone else. I needed to show God that I was ready for promotion. See, integrity and character are the keys to promotion. I'm sure that if I needed a job at that hotel, I could have received one because of my character and commitment to prosper that establishment.

No matter what situation in which you find yourself, you should measure right and wrong by the Word of God because it is your final authority. Let the Word be the gauge of your character. Ask God whether your actions line up with His character. He will show you areas in which you need to improve. Your character should be based on what *God* has determined to be right and wrong. You have to develop this kind of viewpoint if you truly want to discover your destiny.

GO WITH GOD, NOT WITH THE NORM

When I was a child and I wanted to do something my friends were doing, my parents would say, "So if they jumped off a cliff, would you?" Looking back, that statement seems absurd, but it's actually a good question. Are you willing to follow the crowd at the expense of pursuing what God wants for you?

No matter how many people you get to agree with your theory on a particular subject, that still doesn't mean that it's right. You can't make the right decisions based solely on feelings. Before you decide what's right or wrong, check the Word of God. Get a good concordance and research things for yourself. Let your character be molded and shaped by God and His Word.

You'd be surprised how many people leave God out of their decision-making process. Good character requires that you involve Him in everything you do. I've heard men say, "I don't feel that God really minds if I'm living with this woman, just as long as I'm not sleeping with her. I mean, I don't think that God would really have a problem with that." It doesn't really matter what you think—it's what God thinks that matters. And His Word will never change. Godly character is a reflection of what *He* feels is right, not the norms and values of the world or society.

Good character requires that you involve God in everything you do.

Basing your character on society's standards can be disastrous. Societal definitions of what's right and wrong change from one moment to the next. I hear people on talk shows say, "The institution of marriage was good twenty years ago, but times have changed." When people say these things, they don't know how wrong they are. They are responding based on emotions and desires that go against God's Word.

In the book of Genesis, God joined Adam and Eve and commanded them to be fruitful and multiply. So the idea that marriage is outdated is flawed. No matter what the statistics say about the rising divorce rates, you don't *have* to get divorced. Develop in the love of God so that you have the character necessary to sustain your relationship, even when you go through tough times with your spouse. If research companies, talk shows, your friends, and even family begin to see divorce as "normal," you know what you have to do: You have to build your character above that kind of thinking before it takes root in your life.

When I was a teenager, I had an encounter with my father that ended up developing my character. I couldn't understand why my curfew couldn't be extended to two in the morning. After all, parties in my neighborhood didn't start jumping until about 1:30 A.M. But my dad had other feelings about it. Even though he wasn't a man who understood the Bible like you and I do, he knew what was right and wrong based on how he was raised. Like many of us, his character was formed by his parents and their parents, and so on. Consequently, I was also expected to follow his rules, which I thought were old-fashioned. But my dad was very serious about my sisters' and my making curfew. My father was a policeman, and he knew what kind of activity people got into late at night.

No matter how much I tried to debate the issue with my dad, he wouldn't budge. My curfew was midnight—no exceptions. Every time I went to a party, I had to keep up with the time, because I knew if I got home late, I would have to face serious consequences from Big Dollar! In our household, you followed the rules or you suffered the consequences. My father was an imposing figure, and to be honest, I had great respect for him. Usually, all he and my mom had to do was give me a piercing look and I straightened up.

Even though I thought it was perfectly all right to come home at two in the morning, it wasn't right according to my dad's standards. So I had to make adjustments based on his way of doing things, not mine. As I got older, I understood the value of coming home at a decent hour. It provided much more stability than being out all night. My dad taught me how to be disciplined, how to set priorities, and how to submit to authority. He shaped my character.

No matter how ridiculous society may think it is, according to God's standards, it is still fashionable to be a person of character and integrity. Now you may be asking, "Why are you spending so much time on this?" The answer may surprise you. I've taken time to explain what character looks like to help you see that you will never rise above the limitations of your character. Until you get rid of those limits, until you get rid of those flaws in your character, you won't increase in certain areas in your life.

Many of the qualities in your character were shaped by your parents and other influential people in your life. They did the best they could with what they had to help you navigate through this life. If your character is flawed, you have the power to do what it takes to change. God is the ultimate parent, and He wants you to be the best you can be. He'll never take advantage of you or abuse you in any way. If you ask Him to help you with your character, He will. God's Word, especially the book of Proverbs, is a great place to begin learning how to establish good character.

There are people who have the right education, know the right people, and do what they think are the right things, but because of their character issues, they will never taste the level of success that God desires for them. If you find that at the end of every month you have a negative balance in your bank account, you need to examine your character regarding your finances. If you can't find a job, you may need to look at how you're demonstrating character to potential employers. What are you doing that shows God that you're making the most of what He has given you?

I encourage you to examine what you do when no one is looking. Do you live with integrity? When confronted with a morality issue, do you take a stand against what is wrong and embrace the truth of God's Word? Living a life of integrity is going to cost you—anything worth having will. But the benefits far outweigh the price.

Review Nuggets

Character is doing what's right because it's right, and doing it right. Good character leads to success in life. God won't release the fullness of His blessings in your life if your character is bad. How you handle situations that call for good character determines whether you are ready for what God wants to do in and through your life.

Your words, thoughts, feelings, decisions, actions, and habits all shape your character. If you embrace the world's way of speaking, thinking, and acting, your character will ultimately reflect ungodly beliefs, norms, and values. But when you make the Word of God your final authority in life, your character will propel you down the path to lasting prosperity and success.

Foundation Scripture

I am the vine, ye are the branches: He that abideth in me, and I in him, the same bringeth forth much fruit: for without me ye can do nothing.

John 15:5

Practical Application

You demonstrate godly character by doing what's right because it's right. Set yourself up for God to do something special in your life by looking for opportunities to benefit those who have disappointed you. Do something kind for them, and write down your thoughts about it in your journal.

Behind
Closed Doors

Do you remember playing with Play Doh™ as a child? You could shape it and mold it into whatever you wanted! And the Play Doh™ kit came with tools that enabled you to manipulate the dough to look the way you wanted. The point was to use your creativity to shape the dough to your liking.

Likewise, God wants to shape us into the image of His Son, Jesus (Isaiah 64:8). There is a process that we all must go through in order for the character of God to be formed in us. Life's circumstances are the tools God uses to develop godly character in His children.

The Latin word for *character* means "to mold and create." When I think about molding and creating something, I think of clay in the hands of a potter. Take a moment to think about what a potter does and how long it takes him to mold a bowl out of clay. Similarly, character is not something that comes overnight. It is the result of continual obedience to God's Word and His ways of doing things. When obeying God becomes your lifestyle, your character will reflect that.

According to 1 Peter 2:5 we are living stones. We are God's representatives on the Earth. It is for this reason that we must maintain godly character, which includes honor, integrity, truth, gratitude, and modesty. These characteristics should be modeled by Christians, especially those such as parents and leaders, who serve as examples to others.

We are God's representatives on the Earth.

TAKE A STAND

One of the most courageous things you can do to demonstrate character is to take a stand for what is right, even when you know you're
going to be ridiculed and rejected. When you stand for what is right,
people will respect you as a person of excellence, even if their words
and actions don't reveal that to you.

There was a time in my life when I had to take a stand. A high-profile
member of my congregation was going through a bitter divorce, and
the court subpoenaed me because of my private counseling sessions
with him and his wife. That action became public knowledge, and the
media had a field day with me and the church. They questioned my
wealth and my involvement in the case, and wanted to know if I was
going to show up in court.

Now, I could have shown up in court just to get the heat off of myself.
But no matter how I struggled with the media scrutiny, my character
wouldn't allow me to give in. I knew that my counseling sessions were
private and privileged information, and I knew that it wouldn't be right
for me to discuss those things in front of the world. I risked going to jail
for doing what was right. But I knew that I would be risking even more
if I caved in to outside pressure.

Every time you choose to do what's right no matter how unpopular it
may be, you develop the inner strength to withstand the attacks of the
enemy. If we seek godly character by committing to a life of integrity,
power will be added to our lives.

God wants to etch His likeness into your life so that you can be a witness of His love. You are an ambassador of Jesus Christ (2 Corinthians
5:20), His representative on the Earth. The only way that some people
will know the love of God is through *your* life. Whether you know it or
not, people are watching you. If you are known to be a representative

of Jesus but you compromise your moral values and integrity on a daily basis, people aren't going to be drawn to the Lord. God wants your life to impact others for Him and His kingdom.

God wants to bless us with promotion, but we often forfeit those opportunities because of a lack of character. We would rather take the easy way out because we think nobody's watching. Whatever you compromise to keep you will lose. Compromise will lead you away from your destiny. But living a lifestyle of integrity will lead to promotion. It won't always be easy. In fact, there will be times when you will have to risk losing a job or an important relationship to do what you know is right. But even if people call you a "Goody Two-shoes" or "holier than thou," making the commitment to do what's right will always lead to great rewards.

When you feel an intense urge to give in to negative emotions or to go along with the crowd, ask God for the strength to do what's right because it's right. Don't give in to the pressure to be accepted by people. Developing godly character is going to cost you something. You can't decide one day to be a person of integrity and expect to arrive at your destination just like that. Building character is a process, and cultivating integrity is a lifelong experience. You will always be working on it, because going against the flow takes dedication, hard work, and a constant examination of your life.

Developing godly character is going to cost you something.

ARE YOU READY TO PAY THE PRICE?

Luke 14 talks about the price you will have to pay for good character. As you know, Jesus was someone who was in demand on a constant basis. Popular in some people's eyes and despised by others, He ministered the healing, delivering power of God all the time. Naturally, it wasn't long before great crowds of people began following Him. Some had pure motives, while others only wanted to be around Him for their own selfish reasons. But they all wanted a taste of His power.

In Luke 14:26 Jesus said, "If anyone comes to Me and does not hate his [own] father and mother, and wife, and children . . . he cannot be my disciple" (AMP). The Message says it like this, "Anyone who comes to me but refuses to let go of father, mother, spouse, children, brothers, sisters—yes, even one's own self!—can't be my disciple." In other words, if you love people more than you love God, you can't achieve the success He has for you.

Jesus said that you have to give up what you love the most to follow Him. I know this revelation might seem harsh, but let's look at it from a different perspective. God is the Creator of all things, and that includes you and me. When we were growing up, some of us had dreams of becoming doctors, firemen, teachers, and a variety of other occupations. As for me, I wanted to be a professional football player. I began playing when I was very young, and I was good at it. I received accolades from my family, especially my father, and I saw how people respected athletes. If you were good, teams were willing to pay for your winning abilities.

I lived and breathed football from age five or six until my college years. I studied the best teams and the best players and tried to adapt their skills into my game. Before I knew it, I had the attitude as well as the physical stature of a top-rate football player. I wrestled my unsuspecting sisters whenever I got a chance. I received a lot of positive reinforcement from male influences at home and at school. I was on cloud nine. I just knew that I was going to the pros.

What I want you to see here is that my dream began as a mindset. The words I heard at home, from my coach, on television, and from my peers shaped my dream. My emotions, decisions, actions, habits, and character followed. In a sense, I had placed becoming a professional athlete on such a pedestal that it became my god.

Growing up, I never thought about asking God what His plan for my life was. My parents didn't discuss it, and since I was good at football, I naturally gravitated toward it. This dream consumed my very being, and like so many other young African-American males, I knew it was my ticket out of poverty. So you could just imagine my disappointment when I was sidelined for most of my college career because of nagging injuries. My dream of becoming a professional athlete was shattered, and with it, my hope for a bright future.

What I didn't realize at the time was that my dream of becoming a professional athlete was not part of God's destiny for me. Yes, I was good and I had the passion for it. I've said before that passion is the fuel for success, and that is true. But passion alone isn't enough to sustain lifelong success. I am passionate about a lot of things and have talents in many areas, but it was only when my passion for God hooked into my passion to please Him first above everything else that my life began to make sense.

So when Jesus said that you can't be His disciple until you let go of your concept of happiness, He is speaking of your willingness to yield to His higher plan for your life. Out of my ignorance, I was on the road to loving football more than God, and I would have been so unhappy in the end—not because of football per se, but because I wouldn't have found true fulfillment. You see, God placed a special spiritual "hole" in each of us that can be filled only by Him. No matter how many things you acquire, that hole will remain.

Where I once freely gave up my free time to spend hours studying football plays, I decided to put everything aside to study God's Word. And even though I thought I could find success only as a football player, God has provided me with more than enough to accomplish my purpose on this Earth even without football. The inner peace that I spent most of my young life trying to find, I now have.

Pleasing God has become the vehicle to receiving fulfillment in every area of my life. The same goes for you. Be careful not to trust material wealth to give you the success you're looking for. Make a conscious effort to ask God first before you do anything. That's the cost of being His disciple—being willing to follow Him no matter how illogical it may seem.

> *Pleasing God has become the vehicle to receiving*
> *fulfillment in every area of my life.*

In society today, great value is placed on reason and on doing what makes sense by the world's standards. But just because something makes sense to your logical mind doesn't mean it makes for good character, or that it will put you on the path to lasting success. Science is a discipline based on logic. If it can't be calculated with logic, then it can't be true. There are many facts in life, but only one truth, and that is found in the Word of God. A lot of the things God asks you to do—such as showing kindness to your enemies and speaking positively to a challenging situation—will defy common sense. Human logic can go only so far, but God's logic is infinite. It has the answer to every question in the universe, but you must be sincerely committed to His way of doing things to uncover the hidden mysteries of His Word (Matthew 13:44).

As Believers, we are in the process of being transformed into the image of Jesus Christ so that we can love one another unconditionally without reservation. You see, one day we're going to see Him, and we need to look like Him because that's the only evidence that we belong to Him. Just like parents who know their children by the fact that they resemble them in some way, God knows you when you resemble Him.

Your faith and commitment to establishing His character in your life will lead you to a great destiny. But you must make God your absolute priority in life. Scripture says that as you seek God, all that you dream will follow after you (Matthew 6:33).

Scripture says that as you seek God, all that you dream will follow after you.

SEE YOURSELF AS HE SEES YOU

Knowing how God sees you is vital to establishing yourself in the character of Jesus. You have to know who you are. You have to understand that you were made in the image of God Himself (Genesis 1:26, 27). You are God's offspring. God knew you before you were even formed in your mother's womb (Jeremiah 1:5). He gave you a physical body and dominion and authority over everything in the world, including your destiny. Your level of success or failure depends on your recognition of this truth.

When you live a lifestyle of integrity, you allow God's nature to shine and affect this physical realm. When you don't accept the truth that you are God's offspring, you deny your inheritance. You limit your power when you don't accept who you were created to be. You were created to triumph over every challenge and walk effortlessly through life. The day you understand that you were created in the image of God, you are no longer subject to what you see, hear, touch, taste, and smell. You are able to operate according to God's design for you on the Earth.

> *You were created to triumph over every challenge and walk effortlessly through life.*

Now, every Believer has the potential to operate in his full authority on the Earth, but many never realize the fullness of what God planned for them. They remain immature, never cultivating God's character in their lives. They tolerate the enemy's attacks as though they are powerless to do anything about them. But I want to tell you that when it's all said and done, those are the people who will never reach the destiny that God has planned for them. This doesn't mean that God loves them any less. But He will not give someone more responsibility if his character is undeveloped. It would be irresponsible for God to give any of us power that we are not mature enough to handle.

When I was twelve or thirteen, I stole my uncle's car and drove it around the neighborhood because I was confident that I knew how to drive. When my mom found out she said, "Lord have mercy! You drove what?" She was furious with me because I broke the law. It didn't matter that I knew how to drive. That wasn't the point. My birth certificate said that I wasn't the legal age. See, if the police would've caught me, they would have fined my parents for allowing me to drive without a license.

Likewise, your mindset may need to change where character and responsibility are concerned. It doesn't matter how mature you appear to people. The true test is whether the character of Jesus rises up within you when you are faced with a challenge.

Just as it takes time to mature into adulthood, developing character is a process. Until you develop character, you'll continue to allow your thinking, emotions, decisions, actions, and habits to be influenced by sources other than God's Word. Until you develop godly character, you'll never stop being offended. You'll hold grudges against people and respond with unforgiveness. But when you allow God to help you discipline your thought life, your character will begin to change.

WHO ARE YOU WHEN NO ONE IS LOOKING?

What goes on behind closed doors at home? Do you behave one way in public, but another way at home? This is another indicator of your character. Remember that God is always watching you. You can live by rules and regulations, but does your life accurately represent the character of Jesus Christ? In order to have godly character, you must habitually practice what you know is right, even when no one is around.

Compromising your character may give you temporary satisfaction, but you will always end up feeling bad about it on some level. You have to be willing to put your feelings aside to experience God's joy in your life. Your feelings are temporary, but when you choose integrity, you'll experience joy that lasts forever.

The Old Testament law demanded that males be circumcised as a sign of their commitment to God. It was intended to be an outward sign of their internal decision to live a life of integrity. Unfortunately their focus shifted from wanting to please God, to wanting to be seen and praised by others. Jeremiah 9:25 says, "I will punish all who though circumcised [outwardly, in the flesh] are still uncircumcised [in corresponding inward purity]" (AMP). Don't let this be your story. Don't be numbered among those who tell others how they should live, but don't follow those same principles in their own lives (Matthew 23:3–23).

Although the scribes and leaders of Jesus' day knew the law better than anyone, Jesus called them hypocrites. They exalted themselves at the expense of their relationship with God. Jesus commended them on their knowledge of the law, but they neglected the most important principle of doing what's right because it's right. These leaders had little character, and consequently the integrity of Israel as a nation deteriorated as well.

WORK IT OUT

It's not always easy to follow God's instructions. It often requires stepping out in faith without knowing the outcome. It means that you obey God by praying for those who have hurt you. It means forgiving them and speaking well of them. It means waiting on God instead of trying to get back at people. It means doing what God says, no matter what the cost. Having character will challenge your destructive habits and unhealthy decisions. It's up to you to leave these things behind and pursue God like never before, so that you can reach the destination He has for you.

Make the decision today to be a true ambassador for Jesus Christ. When your emotions try to get the best of you, choose to exercise character. Make sure that you don't put anything or anyone else above God. Yield to His instructions, no matter how uncomfortable they might be. Put your feelings aside, and practice doing what's right every day. That's how the character of God will be formed in your life.

Review Nuggets

Character is choosing God's ways over feelings or logic, and it involves being the same behind closed doors as you are in the presence of others. When you cultivate character, you stand up for what is right, even when others don't agree with you. Having godly character positions you to receive more power and spiritual authority from God. He wants to shape you into the image of Jesus Christ. Every time you choose to do what's right, you develop the inner strength to withstand the attacks of the enemy.

Foundation Scripture

I am the Lord, Who practices loving-kindness, judgment, and righteousness in the earth, for in these things I delight.

Jeremiah 9:24 (AMP)

Practical Application

The Word of God encourages us to develop character. We do this by developing the fruit of the Spirit found in Galatians 5:22–23. Take a moment to examine your life. Can you identify areas where your character has been compromised? Take out your journal and write down how you will address those areas and what you will do to develop the fruit of the Spirit in your life.

Grow Into God's Character

Reaching your destiny won't happen just because you have big dreams or strong ambition. You will have to make some serious choices. What many people don't realize is how important it is to *prepare* for God's blessings. Part of that preparation includes remaining connected to Jesus so you can receive and sustain the blessings of God in your life. When you remain connected to the Lord through obedience to His Word and prayer and fellowship with the Holy Spirit, you put yourself in a position to benefit from all that God has for you.

John 15:4 says, "Dwell in Me, and I will dwell in you. [Live in Me, and I will live in you.] Just as no branch can bear fruit of itself without abiding in (being vitally united to) the vine, neither can you bear fruit unless you abide in Me" (AMP). Jesus says that if you remain vitally connected to Him through His Word, He'll dwell in you. This is a promise. Abiding in Jesus will cultivate His personality and character in you. When He has first place in your life and you value spending time with Him more than anything else, He promises that you will get good results in life.

"Bearing fruit" means getting results. Not only does fruit-bearing refer to the fruit of the Spirit—love, joy, peace, longsuffering, gentleness, goodness, faith, meekness, and temperance (Galatians 5:22, 23)—it also refers to the results of your endeavors, gifts, and talents. Whatever it is that God has called you to do, even where your employment is concerned, the fruit is the tangible evidence that God has called you.

Sometimes people try to get results by doing things in their own strength and ability. They resort to the world's tactics to get results without possessing godly character. Situational ethics and "playing the game" are attempts to achieve success outside of God's power and will. Many people figure everything will work out if they have the right connections and know the right things to say and do, but they are wrong. In order to bear *lasting* fruit, you must develop from the inside and let that change be reflected outwardly in your daily life.

Allow God to shape you. Exercise your spiritual muscles by letting situations in life develop your character. Spend time with God. Be a willing vessel, and let Him do the work by giving you the strength to endure and mature (Isaiah 40:31).

> *Exercise your spiritual muscles by letting*
> *situations in life develop your character.*

GROW IN LOVE; GROW IN CHARACTER

Spiritual growth parallels natural growth in many ways. A baby is not physically or emotionally mature enough to handle the same things as an adult or even an older child. For example, if a baby tried to consume whole food too soon, it could die. Its system is not ready to handle it. The same is true of "spiritual infants." There are things God won't release into your life until He knows you are mature enough to handle them. Otherwise, you could destroy yourself.

Growing in character is growing in the love of God. The Bible says that God is love (1 John 4:16). He doesn't just have love, He *is* love. Therefore, His very character reflects love, which includes the nine fruits of the Spirit listed in Galatians 5:22, 23. In order to develop character, you must demonstrate the fruit of the Spirit and apply it to the challenges you face.

I know there are a lot of Christians who are eager to get everything God promised, but just like a baby can't eat whole food until it has developed, you can't expect to dine at the table of God's abundance until you begin to develop the character of love Himself. By allowing God to mold you when you are going through the challenges of life, you will grow in love and character. The more you cultivate the character of God and consistently respond to situations based on the Word of God, the more you will be equipped to handle the blessings.

God is a parent, and as a loving Father, He determines what is best for you and the timing and season in which to release certain blessings. He knows exactly what you need to mature and grow. He will take you through your growth stages gradually so you will be able to successfully arrive at spiritual adulthood. Many people want to rush through the stages of character development, because at times they can be uncomfortable, but it just doesn't work that way.

It is so easy for us to observe our circumstances and say, "Well, this isn't working!" or, "Why hasn't that happened in my life yet?" You can't expect God to fulfill His promises before He's ready. Whatever stage you are in, continue to press toward the goal of growing in the character of God.

It can be frustrating to do what you believe to be right and not get immediate results. If you are honest, if it were left up to you, the will of God in your life would be fulfilled today! If that were the case, though, you wouldn't go through all of the necessary steps of preparation. You may say, "Well, I'm ready." But you may not be truly ready. If you find yourself at this point, be bold. Go to the Lord and ask Him to show you where you need to grow.

Many Christians mistake the length of time they have been born again as a measure of maturity. However, just because you have been saved for a long time doesn't automatically mean you have developed the character of Jesus. Maturity is demonstrated by the decisions you make consistently. More specifically, it is gauged by whether you regularly make decisions that line up with the Word of God.

I've heard people say, "I've been saved for a long time. I've been through this before, and I'm ready for God's blessings." Too often, however, it is these same people whom you hear cursing in the parking lot, speaking negatively outside of the church walls, and yielding to behavior that doesn't reflect godly character. You can be a Christian for twenty years, but if you fail to develop the character of Jesus, which says, "I'll do right even when I'm being done wrong," you're still not ready to receive what God has for you. He will bless you not according to what you think you deserve, but by the measure of your character.

STAY FOCUSED

It's no surprise that in today's microwave society, Believers want instant blessings. Many of us have pressing desires and expect God to fulfill them quickly. We aren't willing to go through the process, and if we are willing, we want to go through it in a hurry. When we don't get what we want, we get frustrated and begin to doubt God's love for us. This causes some people to abandon the destination God has for them.

To avoid frustration and the temptation to quit, you must always remember that there is a due season and an appointed time for everything. Your focus should be on preparing to receive God's best for your life by doing everything necessary to obtain the good life.

For example, God's Word says that wealth and riches are in His plan for your life (Psalm 112:1–3). So in addition to confessing the Scriptures and sowing financial seeds, demonstrate your confidence in God by opening a savings account and being a good steward of the money you have now. Step out on ideas and insights that God gives you, which could be avenues to additional income. Money isn't going to just fall out of the sky! God will show you the things you must do to position yourself for financial increase.

Giving up, caving in, and quitting are not options. Doubt is a reflection of a lack of faith. Stay focused on God as you go through the seasons and phases of spiritual development.

WILL HE RECOGNIZE YOU?

You don't belong to Jesus just because you go to church and can quote a bunch of Scriptures. Riding around with a Jesus bumper sticker doesn't make you a Christian, either. God's Word makes it clear that you know a Christian not by his church attendance or how "holy" he is, but by his fruit. That fruit is his character (Matthew 7:16–20).

Who do you represent when you are not at church—God or the world? You must be God-conscious at all times, not just on Sundays. God has great plans for your life, but in order to walk them out, you must spend time with Him every day. The more time you spend in the Word, praying and basking in God's presence, the more like Jesus you will become. People will be drawn to Him by observing your life.

Consistency in doing the things you know to do, such as prayer, study of the Word, and spending time with God, is a vital key to unlocking your destiny. Be willing to stay where God has put you until it's time to move to the next level. Many people abort their destiny because they haven't received what they want when they want it. They put God on their time-table, and when it doesn't happen according to their schedule, they quit.

> *Consistency in doing the things you know to do, such as prayer, study of the Word, and spending time with God, is a vital key to unlocking your destiny.*

What they don't realize is that when you are impatient, you confirm to God that you aren't ready for the next level. When you're willing to draw a line in the sand and say to God, "I love you so much that I'm willing to let go of my agenda," then He will begin to release more blessing and responsibility to you.

When I first got saved, I served at a Baptist church. I was so on fire for God that I wanted to help in any way I knew how. I volunteered in various areas of the ministry, and whatever the pastor wanted done, I did my best to make it happen. One Saturday morning, I rented a car and showed up at his house. When he asked why I was there, I told him that I wanted to be his chauffeur for the day. I can't tell you how grateful he was that I was willing to give up my day off to help him. I wasn't trying to get noticed by the deacon board; I just wanted to help.

Being faithful in the little things demonstrates your level of character. Do something to help someone, and don't ask for compensation or applause. When you're so committed to God that you surrender your life to Him instead of looking for Him to give you something, that's when God knows His character has been shaped in you.

Character is not about doing goody-goody things to get God to love you more. He couldn't possibly love you more than He already does. Walking in the character of God is a way of life. It's about spending time with Him and developing an intimate relationship with Him. It requires learning how to do what He tells you instead of giving in to your emotions and desires. It's about rooting your thoughts in His character so deeply that the enemy no longer has the ability to move you away from your destiny.

The single objective of your faith is not about how many cars you can obtain, how big your house is, or how much money you have. While God wants you to live prosperously, if you seek Him first, all of these things will be added to your life (Matthew 6:33). The objective of your faith is to transform your life by developing the character of Jesus.

While walking through the process of character development, temptation *will* happen. As they say, opportunity may knock once, but temptation bangs on your door forever. You have to make the decision that God's Word is your final authority and stick to it, no matter what. Establishing boundaries is vital to developing successful character. If you're presently being tempted, decide today to pass the test. God has given you the answers in His Word. Let your character rise above your desire to yield to the enemy's suggestions. Once Satan recognizes that his assaults against your life can't move you from your stance on the Word, he will withdraw from you.

I believe that achieving godly character is the bedrock of living the Christian life. Some of us thought all we had to do was walk down to the altar, repeat the sinner's prayer, and everything would be all right, but there is so much more to salvation than that. First John 3:14 says, "We know that we have passed from death unto life because we love the brethren." The evidence of your salvation is the love of God in your life.

Achieving godly character is the bedrock of living the Christian life.

In order to reach your destiny, character is vitally important. Are you ready to go to the next level? Have you decided to make changes in your words, thoughts, emotions, decisions, actions, and habits so that God's character can be formed in you? Living a lifestyle of integrity sets you up for expansion. It offers stability in your life and proves you can be trusted. Character also gives you the confidence to follow God's plan for your life. Make the choice to do what's right because it's right, and prepare for destination overflow!

*Make the choice to do what's right because it's right,
and prepare for destination overflow!*

Review Nuggets

Developing character is a process that takes time. You can't skip vital stages of spiritual development on your way to your destiny. Preparation is the key to receiving the blessings and promises of God. Even when it seems that things aren't happening as quickly as you'd like, don't give up, cave in, and quit. Remain focused. Allow the pressures and challenges of life to forge God's character in you. Display godly character by walking in love and allowing the fruit of the Spirit to be demonstrated in your life.

Foundation Scripture

But the fruit of the Spirit is love, joy, peace, longsuffering, gentleness, goodness, faith, Meekness, temperance: against such there is no law.

Galatians 5:22–23

Practical Application

In what ways can you allow the fruit of the Spirit to be seen in your life? How can you display godly character and walk in love despite challenges and circumstances? Write your responses to these questions in your journal and use them as a guide for your daily struggles in this area.

Destination:
Higher Level

Your destiny begins with you. Some of you will have to make big decisions in order to reach your destiny. When you submit to God through the process, you give Him the opportunity to shape your destiny, and you have the opportunity to receive all the blessings God has promised.

People who have character know how to do the right thing, no matter what. If you don't have character, God's blessings will be perpetually out of reach. But character will keep you in the will of God.

Jesus had character. Even when people rejected Him, He continued to love them. When He was being nailed to the cross, He asked God to forgive His accusers (Luke 23:34). Remember the man who was crucified next to Jesus? He asked Jesus to remember him when He arrived in paradise. You know, Jesus could have easily taken his pain out on that guy. He could've said, "Man, here I am nailed up to this thing, and you're asking me to remember you? Forget all of you! God, take me off of this cross right now. These people aren't worth it." But He said nothing of the kind. Character allowed the Son of God to be wrongly accused and sentenced to excruciating pain on a splintered cross. Character allowed Him to obey God in the midst of intense agony. He did what was right because He desired to do what God said at any cost. This is the kind of character that enabled Jesus, even while stricken with pain, to say, "This day are ye with Me in Paradise."

It's easy to act on feelings, but you have to remember who you represent. You need to be God-conscious at all times. God has entrusted you with a ministry to reconcile people to Christ. That means you need to spend time with Him so you can reach the destination that will be a witness of His love. People are drawn to God by how you live, not just by your words. They value consistency. One of the most powerful weapons you can use is consistency. Do the right thing when it's right. Love people by being nice to them. If you're rejected, be like Jesus and shake it off. If they want to receive what you have to offer, make yourself available. God watches, waiting to see if, in fact, you're ready to go to a higher level.

Galatians 5 outlines the character we should have. That chapter talks about being patient and gentle and having a life of discipline. In other words, the character of God contains all of these characteristics, and He wants us to mature in these areas. Galatians 5:22 says, "But what happens when we live God's way? He brings gifts into our lives, much the same way that fruit appears in an orchard—things like affection for others, exuberance about life, serenity. We develop a sense of willingness to stick with things, a sense of compassion in the heart, and a conviction that a basic holiness permeates things and people" (The Message). In order to reach the destiny God has designed, you have to love Him enough to obey His Word.

In order to reach the destiny God has designed, you have to love Him enough to obey His Word.

Some people desire power, have a great calling on their life, have great wealth, and believe they have success and joy. They desire God's abilities deep in their hearts, but they have little character. Strategy by itself won't be enough for you to be successful. The Bible says, "The way of transgressors is hard" (Proverbs 13:15). You may know how to do something, but that doesn't necessarily mean that's the thing you ought to be doing at that particular time. Let me tell you, without enough character you might prosper for a while, but because you've disconnected yourself from the root of love, whatever benefits you gain won't last long.

Have you ever seen Christians who achieve success, who appear to be spiritual and in tune with God, but whose lives look like the world? Now I understand why. They've disconnected from the life-giving force of love. That's why a man can get delivered and then slip back into sin after three months. How is it that a woman can be healed of an illness and then die from the same illness later? The world calls it hypocrisy. They think Christians really are no different from them, and in many cases they're right. Unfortunately, many Christians haven't made the decision to become so intimate with God that His character takes over their inclination to sin. See, you can operate the laws and the principles and they will somewhat produce in your life, but if you disconnect from the root of love and disconnect from character, you disconnect from the life-giving force that will cause that thing to remain. I've seen Christians operate in God's laws and get some results, only to see those results spoiled because they're not operating in love. In order to arrive at your destination, you must always evaluate your motives to determine why you do what you do.

The truth is, you'll never rise above the limitations of your character. Life is nothing but a series of decisions, and you create the character you have simply by the choices you make. God gave you the authority to make the choice to live in blessings or failure. Your character is developed with every choice you make. You choose the type of character you want to have. Your choices will help you achieve the success you want.

God gave you the authority to make the choice to live in blessings or failure.

Doing good works doesn't get you into Heaven. God already loves you. You can't buy your salvation by feeding the poor, helping the homeless, or being a celebrated philanthropist. You don't have to read your Bible so God will be pleased with you. The Word of God has been provided to help develop successful character. He is impressed when you choose to do what the Holy Spirit tells you. You do what is right out of appreciation for what Jesus did for you on the cross, and that motivates you to make choices in line with His Word.

Now, when you achieve that level of confidence in God, failure is not an option. Heaven will always back you up. You, too, can achieve this level of confidence in what God can do for you, but you must plan to have that kind of success. You have to schedule time in the Word of God and learn what it says about you. Once you're confident in the truth that you have a blood-bought right to claim every promise in His Word, choose two or three Scriptures and begin to meditate on them. The first chapter of the book of Joshua clearly outlines how to arrive at success. Verse 8 says, "This book of the law shall not depart out of thy mouth; but thou shalt meditate therein day and night, that thou mayest observe to do according to all that is written therein: for then thou shalt make thy way prosperous, and then thou shalt have good success." You have the power to make your way prosperous. You have to decide that you want to succeed and do something about it.

> *You have the power to make your way prosperous. You have to decide that you want to succeed and do something about it.*

Meditating on the Word of God will eventually release power into your life. To meditate means to ponder, rehearse, and mutter over. If you were to meditate on Joshua 1:8 by spending time pondering and speaking what God has said, that Word would become so big in you that it would burst forth as power. You would receive insight and empowerment for what you desire in your life. But you have to stick with it. You can't quit after two days or even a week. No matter what you see or hear, you have to remain consistent. Just like a weightlifter, you have to condition your mind and heart to receive from God. It's not an overnight process. If it were, it would be unhealthy. I encourage you to spend time with a specific Scripture for a month, with the faith to believe that God will do something great in your life. Attach that Scripture to an action, a particular thing that you desire, and meditate on until it brings forth the fruit that you desire.

In this part of the book, we've looked at how living in integrity leads to our destiny. The next section will focus on important truths about reaching your God-given destination and determining what you've been put on this Earth to do. Everyone has been given an innate gift to do something unique that no one else can do. There are many roads to your future, but I encourage you to select the one that leads to your destiny. I tell you, there is nothing like discovering what you've been created to do. You enjoy a sense of peace and fulfillment that only God can give. Let the next section inspire you to change and discover the race that has been set just for you.

There are many roads to your future, but I encourage you to select the one that leads to your destiny.

Review Nuggets

Developing character is a process that takes time. Don't avoid the process. Go through it with a positive attitude. Don't try to change by your own strength. To enjoy that lasting fruit, rely on God to change you first on the inside!

Foundation Scripture

But they that wait upon the LORD shall renew their strength; they shall mount up with wings as eagles; they shall run, and not be weary; and they shall walk, and not faint.

Isaiah 40:31

Practical Application

How have you developed stronger character through reading this book and doing the exercises? What are other ways you plan to develop character? What actions are you taking to reach these goals? Write your responses in your journal, and compare them to your previous entries.

Step 8

Embrace Your Destiny

Destination Overflow: God's Will for Your Life

It is God's will for you to live an abundant and prosperous life overflowing with His goodness. I know that may sound extravagant, but that's the kind of God we serve—an overflowing, "too-much" Father who wants to give you His best. Living from paycheck to paycheck, being at the mercy of sickness and disease, and living with a constant sense of fear or worry is not God's plan for you. He sent Jesus so you could experience His overflow and have more than enough provision to meet not only your needs, but also the needs of others. God wants you to enjoy the pleasures of peace, happiness, and fulfillment in every area of your life. This is His perfect will for you. This is "destination overflow."

Many people have bought into the lie that God somehow gets glory when they struggle. Contrary to what some religious people say, being broke, busted, and disgusted does nothing except make a person feel worse about his situation. It causes a sense of hopelessness. It is not God's will for His people to have terrible marriages, rebellious children, bad health, and financial problems. That's Satan's plan. God has given every Believer the right and authority to speak change over his situation in faith. However, if you don't take action by lining up your words and actions with God's Word, your life will remain the same, year after year.

I know how it feels to struggle from paycheck to paycheck, to be stressed out, depressed, and wondering how you're going to make it.

But I have good news: it is the will of God for you to experience destination overflow—a taste of Heaven on Earth!

Look at Jesus' words in John 10:7–10:

> Then said Jesus unto them again, Verily, verily, I say unto you, I am the door of the sheep. All that ever came before me are thieves and robbers: but the sheep did not hear them. I am the door: by me if any man enter in, he shall be saved, and shall go in and out, and find pasture. The thief cometh not, but for to steal, and to kill, and to destroy: I am come that they might have life, and that they might have it more abundantly.

The first lesson from this Scripture is that Jesus is the only way to access the abundant life. That means you must be born again in order to partake of the blessings of the Kingdom of God. Any other means of prosperity is temporary, giving you a false sense of security. Jesus promises total peace and security when you accept Him as your Lord and Savior.

Jesus is the only way to access the abundant life.

The second critical aspect of this Scripture is that *Satan*, not God, is the author of destruction. The devil is the thief who comes to steal from you, kill your destiny, and destroy your life. So many times, religion has painted a picture of God as some kind of ogre who is waiting to strike you down with a lightning bolt when you mess up. Many religious people suggest that God punishes us by serving us a plate of disappointment and distress, but that's not His agenda at all. He wants to do good things for you and make you happy! Jesus assures us in this Scripture that the reason He came to Earth is to provide us with an overflowing, abundant life.

POSITION YOURSELF FOR OVERFLOW

Nothing just happens. Whether good or bad, your life is the result of the seeds you've sown through your thoughts, words, and actions. Your

Word-based choices will put you in position to receive the overflowing good life that God has predestined for you. However, when your thinking, emotions, decisions, actions, habits, and character aren't aligned with God's Word, disappointment and frustration are the result.

> *Your Word-based choices will put you in position to receive the overflowing good life that God has predestined for you.*

1. Get rooted.

The first key to positioning yourself for overflow is to become rooted and grounded in the Word of God. It *has* to be your foundation. This has to be a settled issue in your life. The Word is the origin of all prosperity and abundance, so if you haven't made a decision to make the Word the final authority, don't expect to experience the benefits that it provides.

> *The Word is the origin of all prosperity and abundance.*

Getting rooted in God's Word means you choose to allow biblical principles and teachings to take root in your heart and change your thinking. This comes only through continual meditation, fellowship with God, and application. As you diligently apply these efforts, they will become your standards for living.

2. Change your mindset.

Allowing the Word to take root in your heart and mind will bring you to the next step on your way to destination overflow—a changed mindset. The way you think determines where you will go in life. When your thinking is based on the Word of God, your whole outlook on life will change. If you ever thought poverty was a lifestyle you had to accept, let that old way of thinking go. Transform your thinking to line up with the truth: God takes *pleasure* in your prosperity (Psalm 35:27).

Maybe you used to worry that if ever you were diagnosed with a terminal illness, death would be your inevitable end. Once you get in the Word, however, and see what God has to say about sickness and disease, your thinking will change to accept the reality that by the stripes of Jesus Christ, you have *already* been healed (Isaiah 53:5). Renewing your mind to line up with the Bible is the foundation of all success in life. After changing your mindset, the next area that will follow is your emotions. When your thinking changes, your emotions change as well.

> *Renewing your mind to line up with the Bible is the foundation of all success in life.*

Think about it for a minute. When your feelings are totally out of control, it is generally because of some faulty line of thinking about a particular situation. What you have been meditating on is often the key to why you feel the way you do. When your thoughts are not submitted to the Word of God, your feelings won't be submitted, either. That is why we must allow the Word to completely take over and govern our thinking. When situations come up that go against what the Bible says, don't let those scenarios get past the "checkpoint" of your Word-controlled mind. Guard your mind *first,* and your emotions will follow.

For example, you may have received an eviction notice because you don't have the money to pay the rent. At the point of receiving that notice, you have one of two choices: you can (1) look at your situation through your natural senses and start panicking and speaking words of fear, doubt, and unbelief; or you can (2) immediately switch your thinking into "Word-mode" and go to the Bible to find out what God has to say about it.

According to Philippians 4:19, God will supply all your needs according to His riches in glory. When you meditate on this truth and think about how Heaven's resources can more than take care of your need, you won't *feel* as bad about the situation. And while you will have to fight the temptation to yield to negative emotions, you will remember that God's Word is the *truth* that overrides any *fact* in the natural.

As you harness your emotions and bring them into subjection to the Word, your decisions and actions will follow suit. Consistent repeated actions will form your habits and eventually create the character by which others will know and recognize you.

Character is the determining factor that will demonstrate whether you are ready to handle the blessings, power, and authority in which God wants you to operate. A person can have talents, abilities, and even spiritual gifts, but if his or her character doesn't reflect the character of Jesus, none of those things will matter.

Is the Word governing your thoughts, emotions, decisions, actions, and habits? Maybe the reason things aren't working is because you need to make some adjustments. Begin with the Word and go from there.

PLANT GOOD SEED IN GOOD GROUND

Whatever it is you want to accomplish in your life, it must be based on the Word of God if you want to succeed. First of all, if God didn't assign you the task, it won't produce any fruit. Make sure that every endeavor you take on can be traced back to a Word from God, either from His written Word or words spoken to your spirit.

I've often said that every failure in life is a prayer failure, but I also know that when you don't make the Word your foundation, things will fail. For example, if you are starting a new relationship, make sure you are doing it according to the Word of God. This means sticking close to the guidelines the Bible has set for how Christian men and women should get to know each other. Similarly, if you are launching a new business, find Scripture to plant the godly vision for your business in your mind and heart. Conduct your business with others according to biblical principles of sowing and reaping, and you will see increase.

Why would God want every Believer to start with the Word? I want to remind you that *He* started everything with His Word. God spoke the worlds into existence, and the Scripture says all things are upheld by the Word of His power (Hebrews 1:3). His Word is the prevailing force that should uphold *everything* in your life. First Peter 1:23 says the Word of God is *incorruptible seed*. That means it will always produce a crop—without fail. When you plant the seed of the Word of God in your heart, everything from that point will succeed and prosper. His Word is your guarantee. You don't have to worry about failure when you build your life on the foundation of God's Word.

The second part of this equation I want you to understand is that, while the Word is your "bag of seed," *you* are the ground in which that seed needs to be planted in order to reap a harvest. Seed not planted will not grow and produce. In the same way, the Word-seed left on the pages of the Bible without ever being planted in your heart won't produce the abundant life. It has to go down deep into your spirit and be allowed to take root.

Again, *you* are the ground for the Word of God. And not only are you the ground for the Word of God, you are the ground for words, period. Just like there are words that come from the Kingdom of God and Heaven, there are also words Satan wants to plant in your heart and mind to get you to grow a bad life.

Many marriages are being destroyed by the enemy right now because husbands and wives are listening to the wrong words. Instead of taking the time to find out what God has to say about how they should treat one another or how to resolve conflict, they are listening to the words of popular talk show hosts or well-meaning friends and family. I'm sorry, but if what you are hearing isn't lining up with the Word, it is nothing more than a recipe for disaster. If you purpose to receive God's words, then you'll receive God-seed that will produce the God-kind of abundant life.

Your life is the harvest of the words you have spoken and received. If your father told you that you would never amount to anything, and all you ever heard growing up were negative words spoken to or about you, then you probably grew up believing those things about yourself.

However, with the Word at your disposal, you can create a new reality for yourself by planting the Scripture in your heart.

Sometimes it takes removing yourself from the comfortable and familiar in order to start receiving the words necessary to bring you into the good life. God told Abraham to leave his familiar surroundings and go to a place he had never been. God knew that Abraham's family was framing the way he thought, and that he would never reach his destiny listening to their words. In order to bring Abraham to a place of faith, God had to get him into a position where the only words he heard were from the Father. As a result of his obedience, Abraham prospered and became the "father of many nations" (Genesis 17:5).

So then, the first thing you need to do is take that Word and plant it in your heart. Whether it is in the area of finances, relationships, or healing, find out what God has said about your situation. You do that by reading, listening to, and speaking the Word. Continually confessing the Word will plant it in your heart and give you an inner image of what you are trying to create for yourself. Once that seed takes root, you can't be stopped and you won't be far from reaching destination overflow.

THE LAW OF MEDITATION

Meditation is often misunderstood to be spooky or mystical. Actually, meditation is simply pondering something and turning it over in your mind until you get full understanding and revelation from it. Meditation on the Word of God is the key to success in life.

Meditation on the Word of God is the key to success in life.

Prayer is essential to a successful Christian walk, but meditation adds another dimension to prayer that will take you even further. Joshua 1:8 says,

This book of the law shall not depart out of thy mouth; but thou shalt meditate therein day and night, that thou mayest observe to do according to all that is written therein: for then thou shalt make thy way prosperous, and then thou shalt have good success.

As I've said, I like to look at meditation as "squeezing the juice" out of a Scripture. God associates both prosperity and success with meditation. Prosperity is more than just having a lot of money; it is having enough resources to do what God has told you to do. It is having enough to meet your needs *and* the needs of others. When you are prospering, you are excelling in the things of God and reaching the goals that He has set for you to reach.

Don't let anyone convince you that God wants you poor, or that when you are scraping and struggling you are pleasing the Father. God wants to bless you so you can be a blessing to others, just like Abraham was. Get into His Word and meditate on it so He can show you how to deal wisely in life.

Destination overflow can be a reality in your life when you realize that it isn't about you! Overflow is about ministering to those who are in darkness—who don't know Jesus Christ. God's ultimate purpose for blessing you with the abundant life is so that He can further His great soul-winning plan in these Last Days. The more overflow people see in your life, the better witness you are to those who are crying out for His love.

There is nothing more fulfilling than being able to obey God the moment He tells you to give a certain amount of money to someone who really needs it. When you have enough resources to become a distribution center for others, you demonstrate God's commission for you to be a blessing until all families of the Earth are blessed (Genesis 12:3). Your family is waiting for you to arrive at your final destination so you can show them who God really is.

Remember, the Word-seed is what governs increase in the Kingdom of God. It is the highway to the world of wealth. The more Word you have inside of you, the more increase you will see. It is the gateway to heavenly blessings.

You don't have to struggle and strain through life another minute.

You have sixty-six books of seed that God is waiting for you to plant in your heart. Let the Word change the course of your life and get you on the path to destination overflow; it is His will. No matter what your station, the Word can change you from the inside out. Start meditating on it every day. Destination overflow is just one seed away!

The Word can change you from the inside out.

Review Nuggets

It is God's will for you to live an abundant, prosperous life that is overflowing with His goodness. He sent Jesus specifically for that purpose. However, you must position yourself to receive that overflow. Evaluate your decisions and actions so you can avoid any hindrances that may prevent you from this total experience. Make sure you are always planting good seed in good soil to produce your desired harvest. Spend valuable time in the Word and in meditation. These are key to your success!

Foundation Scripture

The thief cometh not, but for to steal, and to kill, and to destroy: I am come that they might have life, and that they might have it more abundantly.

John 10:10

Practical Application

God desires for you to live abundantly in every area of your life. Take some time to write down your definition of *abundance*. List areas of your life in which you desire to see increase. Begin to meditate on specific Scriptures until you see yourself walking in prosperity.

Reflections of the Father's Love

Do you remember what it was like growing up? Some of you had a loving father in your home, and others did not. Even if you didn't have the type of dad who spent a lot of time pouring into your life, your heavenly Father wants to demonstrate His love for you in more ways than you can imagine. He wants to shower you with His goodness so you can testify of His mercy and loving-kindness to others. That's just the kind of God He is!

While growing up, I really looked up to my father. He was a strong provider for our family, and he taught me a lot about responsibility. I know that even in the midst of hard times, he always did his best to provide for us. While your earthly father's provision can only do so much, God's provision for you far outweighs your earthly father's abilities. God loves you so much, and wants you to experience good things every day because you are His child. Once you know and believe this about your heavenly Father, you will experience amazing peace.

In her syndicated newspaper column, "My Day," Eleanor Roosevelt described such peace as "the kind of calm that comes when one has done the best one can." When you have put into practice the eight steps presented in this book—making the Word your final authority, allowing it to produce your thoughts, emotions, decisions, actions, healthy habits, godly character, and embracing your destiny—you can live life with the confidence that God will take care of the rest. You don't have to worry about the circumstances that surround you, because the Word of God says that nothing can by any means harm you (Luke 10:19)!

MUCH MORE THAN MONEY

Contrary to what you may have learned growing up in church, prosperity is more than just money. While it does include money and material possessions, it goes far beyond those things. It is an expression of God's love for His children.

Many preachers don't talk about money because they have it confused with *materialism*. Those who are materialistic try to solve spiritual problems with material things. They think that acquiring more material goods will somehow bring total happiness to their lives. The Bible says *the love of money* is the root of all evil (1 Timothy 6:10). Money in and of itself is not bad. God uses money to bless His children. The Word of God tells us God blesses us to be a blessing to others. Therefore, as we are blessed, He uses us as distribution centers to bless other people (Genesis 12:2, 3).

Prosperity is having enough to do what God has purposed for you to do, and more. When you are prosperous, you have the ability to bless others. Can you imagine having enough money and material resources that you are able to give a home, a car, or any given amount of money into the life of someone who really needs it? It is an awesome experience to be able to obey God by giving what He tells you to give, when and where He directs you to give it. When you are living in lack and poverty, with barely enough to take care of your own needs, you can't be much help to anyone else. *This is not the will of God.*

When you are prosperous, you have the ability to bless others.

When God put the vision for World Changers Church International in my heart, I had no idea how it would happen. He already knew that I would need *billions* of dollars in order for the fullness of this ministry to become a reality and impact the lives of people around the world. From television broadcasts to hundreds of outreach programs, prosperity is the key to reaching people with the Gospel. Living with just enough to make it from day to day won't fulfill God's plan. What has God destined you to do? Whatever the assignment, you will require resources to accomplish it.

POVERTY IS A MINDSET

Society describes *poverty* as living with little to no money, resources, or means. Homelessness is an extreme version of poverty that many people deal with or have faced at one time or another in their lives. Many people are born into poverty; however, that doesn't mean they have to stay there. There are alternatives available to you. Much like any other thought process, the poverty mindset can be changed. It will take the Word of God to transform this thinking.

Matthew 11:5 describes the results of Jesus' ministry: "The blind receive their sight, and the lame walk, the lepers are cleansed, and the deaf hear, the dead are raised up, and the poor have the gospel preached to them." Poor people need more than mere handouts; they need the Good News that Jesus came to set them free. They need to know without a shadow of a doubt that it is not God's will for them to be poor in *any* area.

Poverty doesn't always mean just a lack of finances. Think of someone who is physically sick but has a lot of money in the bank. While this individual may have money, he is still poor when it comes to physical health. Or imagine someone in great physical health, living a healthy lifestyle, who has a troubled marriage. That person is poor in his marital relationship. These examples illustrate that poverty isn't always a lack of finances. It can exist in any aspect of life.

This isn't God's plan for you. *Whoever* you are, you should be living life in abundance, to the full, until it overflows. This type of lifestyle comes from totally submitting to the Word of God. The Word is the origin of all prosperity. Everything starts with the Bible, and walking these eight steps will get you to the destination God has prepared for you.

Whoever you are, you should be living life in abundance, to the full, until it overflows.

MAKE THINGS HAPPEN

No matter what situation you are facing right now, a solution can be found in God's Word. Whether you need healing, deliverance, or a financial breakthrough, the first step is to find out what God says about it. Then allow His truth to penetrate and change your thoughts.

Third John 1:2 says, "Beloved, I wish above all things that thou mayest prosper and be in health, even as thy soul prospereth." Your soul includes your mind, will, and emotions. According to this Scripture, this is where everything begins. When you have a prosperous soul, your health and circumstances will likewise reflect that. If you want something in your life to change, reprogram your thinking with the Word.

Are you dealing with sickness in your body? The Word of God is the origin of prosperity for you to receive healing. Find out what the Scripture says to appropriate its promises. The truth is God wants you to live a healthy and wealthy life. In Luke 4:18, 19, Jesus clearly describes His mission when He says, "The Spirit of the Lord is upon me, because he hath anointed me to preach the gospel to the poor; he hath sent me to heal the brokenhearted, to preach deliverance to the captives, and recovering of sight to the blind, to set at liberty them that are bruised, To preach the acceptable year of the Lord." If you are struggling in any of the areas mentioned in this Scripture, then Jesus is the solution to your problem! However, it takes receiving *Him* and what *He* has come to do in order for you to experience the healing and deliverance you need.

THE HEAVY WEIGHT

God's Word is the origin of abundance and the very foundation upon which a prosperous life is established. Honoring God's Word *above any other* word puts you in a position to receive overflow. Any time you allow His Word to receive greater honor or weight than anything else, you set yourself up for Him to honor you. When you *honor* something, you treat it with respect and hold it in high esteem. The Word has to be respected and esteemed highly in your life if you want to get to destination overflow.

Let me illustrate by examining marriage relationships. When you enter into covenant with your spouse, you are making a commitment to that person and to God that you will honor her for the rest of your life. That means that you put her needs above your own and you hold her in high regard; higher than anyone else with whom you have a relationship. When you honor your spouse, you don't talk to her in a degrading manner or disrespect her rights as your spouse. You can't say you esteem your spouse if you give more priority to hanging out with your friends or even to watching television when you know that your spouse needs quality time with you. Honor calls for you to put aside other people and things for the sake of your marriage relationship.

The same is true regarding your relationship with God and His Word. You can't say you honor the Word, and then run to other people for advice before you seek out what the Word has to say when you have problems. You can't say you honor God, and then fail to demonstrate that with your resources. You are not honoring God if you disobey His Word in *any area* of your life! If you want the blessing of God, His Word has to be the "heavy weight" in your life.

The Word, not money, holds the key that grants access to the doors of heavenly blessings. It's the seed that controls everything you endeavor to do. Finding out what the Word of God says gives you the tools to begin building abundance in your life.

The Word, not money, holds the key that grants access to the doors of heavenly blessings.

Some people think they don't have a right to the life of abundance that God has prepared for them. God is in covenant with you through Jesus; therefore, you have access to everything He promises in His Word—divine healing, financial prosperity, a prosperous marriage, blessed children, a saved family, and long life (Galatians 3:29)!

BELIEVE YOUR WAY INTO ABUNDANCE

Once you understand that God has provided access to the good life through the covenant, there are four primary action steps you must take. Obtaining the good things God wants to give requires action on your part. You must renew your thinking to gain access to the abundance God has predestined for you.

The first action step is to know and believe that God has a plan and a destiny for your life. To come into your destiny, it's imperative that you believe God has strategically prepared a path for your life that you are to walk in. In order to reach your final destination, you have to trust and believe this. As a child, maybe you were made to feel less than valuable. Were you told that you were a mistake or that you would never amount to anything? That simply isn't true. God is not a respecter of persons—we are all equal. If you apply the principles of prosperity, prosperity will come. In other words, God's rules don't work for some and not for others. In order to find and discover the place God intends for you to be, you must get to the point of believing there is a *specific plan* and a *destiny* for your life.

The second action step is to believe that God, not circumstances, is in control. Whatever you allow inside you will ultimately control you. For instance, if you let negative thoughts dominate your mind, then those negative thoughts will control your life. You don't have to allow yourself to be controlled by your circumstances. Reading and meditating on the Word will infuse your thinking with God's words. Actively examine it from every possible angle. Once you have achieved a level of understanding of His Word, it's easier to envision the great things He has for you.

The third action step is to believe that when you give your best, you will receive God's best. Giving your best gets you the best! Have you been giving mediocre efforts or your absolute best? Doing your best places you in a position to reap a harvest. The Bible says that you reap what you sow (Galatians 6:7). There is absolutely no way you can give your best without getting the best in return. One way God shows His love toward His children is by giving them His best.

There is absolutely no way you can give your best without getting the best in return.

The fourth action step is to keep your priorities in line with God's will to maintain balance and order. In other words, make sure you are doing things according to the Word of God. When you align your priorities with God's Word, you will discover your destiny in life. Nothing happens in your life by accident. In Jeremiah 1:5, the Bible says, "Before I formed thee in the belly I knew thee; and before thou camest forth out of the womb I sanctified thee, and I ordained thee a prophet unto the nations." God was letting Jeremiah know that what he was about to do wasn't a mistake, and that it wasn't because of happenstance. Instead, God revealed to Jeremiah what was in His heart and mind all along. So what God is saying about you is, before you were even formed in your mother's womb, He had already set up a plan, destiny, and purpose for your life!

Before you were even formed in your mother's womb, God had already set up a plan, destiny, and purpose for your life!

NO GREATER LOVE

No matter what you may have done in your life, God loves you. He doesn't *have* love; He *is* love (1 John 4:8). When you develop confidence in His love, the storms of life won't shake you. Your enemies won't faze you. No matter what opposition may come, you can rise to the top every time! Believe God for the abundant life. Hebrews 10:35 says to make sure you don't throw away your confidence, as it will be rewarded. Never doubt God's love for you.

*No matter what opposition may come, you
can rise to the top every time!*

There have been plenty of times in my life when I wanted to quit. I have faced negative reports from the doctor, and financial situations that looked impossible. However, God always brought me through, no matter how it looked. Even though my mind spoke very loudly, my spirit remained rooted in the promises of God. I had confidence in Him as my only source, and I knew that, somehow, the situation would be handled if I stayed in faith and refused to bow to the pressures of the enemy.

Has God spoken a word to your heart? Has He given you a dream or vision that has not yet come to fruition? He may have told you something awesome that you are going to do for His Kingdom, something that will propel you into a life of overflowing abundance, and it looks like the odds are against you. Don't be discouraged. If you can see it by faith, you *can* have it.

God's Word is your covenant platform for prosperity, and when you make the Bible your strong foundation, nothing the enemy tries to do to you will succeed. Walk in the confidence that if God said it, He will do it. If He spoke it, He *will* bring it to pass. It is your heavenly Father's good pleasure to fulfill your dreams and make sure you live a prosperous life. He has provided the tools you need to access it. You can begin creating your good life today!

*It is your heavenly Father's good pleasure to fulfill your
dreams and make sure you live a prosperous life.*

Review Nuggets

Your heavenly Father desires to demonstrate His devoted love to you. God doesn't *give* love, He *is* love. And because He is love, He is waiting to shower you with His goodness. This goes far beyond material things. When you receive God's prosperity plan for your life, it includes total health and wellness in every area of your life. It includes good physical health, financial health, well-being in your marriage, and success in all your relationships.

Don't allow yourself to be bound any longer by materialistic attitudes. Refuse to accept the mindset of poverty. God gave you an imagination so you could imagine yourself doing and having what He says. When you allow the Word to penetrate your thinking and change your inner image of yourself, you are well on your way to fulfilling God's plan!

Foundation Scripture

The Spirit of the Lord is upon me, because he hath anointed me to preach the gospel to the poor; he hath sent me to heal the brokenhearted, to preach deliverance to the captives, and recovering of sight to the blind, to set at liberty them that are bruised, To preach the acceptable year of the Lord.

Luke 4:18–19

Practical Application

The only way to develop confidence in God's Word is to spend time reading and meditating on it. Believe God for what His Word says. Repeat these words:

> I believe God has a specific plan and destiny for my life. Regardless of what I may have been told as a child, I know that I am not a mistake. I have a purpose and will follow the steps necessary to align with the destiny for my life!

Repeat that declaration anytime you begin to feel doubt and unbelief trying to penetrate your thoughts. Next, make a short list of things from God's Word you would like to see manifested in your life. Read and believe the Scriptures that correlate to them. Once you have internalized those Words, take action. Do something to demonstrate your faith in God and His Word!

Discover Your Destiny!

One of the most common questions people ask themselves and God is, *What is my purpose; what was I put on Earth to do?* Unfortunately, many people go through their entire lives never accomplishing what they were put here to do. They end up living empty, frustrated existences. While God wants you to have a job so you can pay your bills and take care of your needs, working a nine-to-five job and retiring when you are sixty-five is not God's definition of a fulfilling life. Your job is not your source. It is a way for you to have money to sow into the Kingdom of God so that you can increase. God doesn't want you to be dependent solely on your job to make it. He has something much greater planned for your life, and it is up to you to discover that plan.

Your success in life is directly connected to your purpose and destiny. Did you know there is something *specific* that God has for you to do? He has put certain gifts and abilities inside you that He wants you to use to reach others. When you are walking in your purpose and your destiny, fulfillment is assured.

When you are walking in your purpose and your destiny, fulfillment is assured.

God wants you to have more than enough to meet your needs and the needs of others. True prosperity is success in *every* area of your life, not just finances. Jesus came to Earth to make this type of life available to you

(John 10:10). He wants you to live a life that is rich, an exceeding-measure type of life, something above the ordinary—plentiful and fully overflowing. You should begin planning *now* for your life of abundant living!

GET IN POSITION

God indeed has a plan and destiny for your life. You were not just randomly given life so you could live an ordinary existence. God has a *specific* plan and purpose for you. If you are ever going to reach your destination, you've got to believe this truth. You have to begin retraining your mind to think, *There is a plan and destiny for my life, and God wants me to discover it!*

Ephesians 2:10 in The Amplified Bible says:

For we are God's [own] handiwork (His workmanship), recreated in Christ Jesus, [born anew] that we may do those good works which God predestined (planned beforehand) for us [taking paths which He prepared ahead of time], that we should walk in them [living the good life which He prearranged and made ready for us to live].

The Word makes it very clear that God has a specific plan for you. There should be no doubt in your mind about that. Once you accept Jesus as your Lord and Savior, you have taken the first step toward God's divine plan for you. He is the access door through which everything else will become a reality. The paths He has for you to take have already been prepared. All you have to do is walk in them, and they will automatically lead you to the good life.

The second truth you need to know is that you must believe God's promises, not the circumstances that surround you. Many Believers pay more attention to what their physical senses are telling them than to what God has said in His Word. Christians have Jesus, through the power of the Holy Spirit, living inside of them, and they have the Word of God. When you meditate on the Word, receive it into your heart, and begin speaking to your circumstances, your circumstances will change.

If you allow the negative impressions, perspectives, and words of the world to undermine the Word of God in your spirit, you will start believing those things rather than seeing things from Heaven's perspective. You can't afford to take the world's suggestions on how to handle situations.

Have you ever thought about the word *circumstance?* Often we hear people say they are surrounded by their circumstance. It makes sense, then, to say that your circumstance is the circle in which you are standing. What specific circle are you standing in? In the natural, it may look like you are standing in a circle of debt, oppression, or frustration, but what does the Word say about your situation? You can change the type of circle you are standing in when you believe that greater is He, Jesus, that is in you than he, Satan, that is in the world. It doesn't matter how many times you hear a preacher tell you that; it has to become a reality to *you.*

> *Greater is He, Jesus, that is in you than he,*
> *Satan, that is in the world.*

The third truth is that if you give the best, you will have the best. Nothing of value will come into being in your life without hard work, persistence, and a commitment to excellence in all that you do. Paying attention to details produces superior performance that positions you for promotion. You have to give 100 percent to God if you want to receive His best. That means obeying Him and developing character, which is doing what's right because it's right. You know in your heart when you are not going all out for God. You know when you are putting a half-hearted effort into the things God has entrusted to you. It is time to take a look at your life and examine whether you are truly giving God your best, or just giving an average effort.

God will not move you to the next level until you master the level you are at now. What was the last thing He told you to do? Have you given it your all, or have you simply skated by, doing the bare minimum? Galatians 6:7 says, "Be not deceived; God is not mocked: for whatsoever a man soweth, that shall he also reap." God is looking at everything to determine whether you can handle the next phase of His blessing. When you give Him your best, He will also give you His best.

Walking in your divine destiny involves ordering your life in a balanced way so that you keep your priorities in line with God's will. God's will is His Word, and when you allow the Word of God to take precedence over every situation you face and seek Him *first* in everything you do, you will find yourself propelled along the path to your destiny.

Psalm 139:16 in The Amplified Bible says, "Your eyes saw my unformed substance, and in Your book all the days [of my life] were written before ever they took shape, when as yet there was none of them." God has a specific path for you to take in life, and once you have positioned yourself to know that path through these four truths, it is simply a matter of walking it out.

Many people get caught up in what *they* want to do instead of finding out what *God* wants them to do. That's why people waste years pursuing endeavors God hasn't called them to undertake, and then get frustrated and blame Him when things don't work out. However, they didn't seek God's wisdom on what they were trying to do! Before stepping out, seek God first. That demonstrates your first priority—fulfilling God's will, not your own.

There is a time and a season for every purpose (Ecclesiastes 3:1). God has developed the master plan for your life, and He knows exactly when you and your purpose need to show up. He is all about reaching people, and when you achieve your destiny, the people God has called you to reach will be impacted forever.

EIGHT STEPS TO GOD'S WILL

Not only are there eight steps to the life you want, but there are also eight steps to discovering the perfect will of God. Here they are:

1. Discover the real desire of your heart.

In discovering your destiny, ask yourself, *What is the real desire of my heart?* What is it that you have always wanted to do? Whether you realize it or not, God has a lot to do with the desires that are planted in your heart. This is not the same as fantasy. Your true desire is that thing you can't get away from no matter how hard you try. Everything you do seems to point to this desire. It is the desire that you had before you found out that it wasn't cool, according to other people's standards. Locate this desire, and you have taken the first step toward your destiny.

2. Determine what stirs your passion.

What stirs your passion? What is that activity you could do all day, every day, no matter how tired you are? What is that thing that gets you so excited and passionate, you can hardly stand it? What is it that you would do even if you didn't get paid for it? It may be teaching, baking cakes, or encouraging others when they are feeling down. You may be a person who loves solving problems or being involved with community work. Whatever that drive is, it is an indication of what God wants you to do.

3. Identify the gifts, anointings, and talents that flow through you naturally.

What are the gifts and talents that flow through you naturally—those things that you are good at that are effortless for you? For someone else, these particular things may be hard work, but they are easy for you. Not only are they easy for you, but you love doing them! You could do them in your sleep, if it came down to it. I can preach a sermon and give you the text and title with my eyes closed. It is embedded in me, and I've been gifted to bring understanding to God's Word. What is it that you can do effortlessly and enjoyably?

Please understand that just because a person is *talented* doesn't mean that there is an anointing, or an enablement, from God to set people free from the oppression of the enemy. There are many singers and entertainers who are talented, but when people leave their concerts, while they were thoroughly entertained, they still leave with the same problems and cares they came in with. When God has *anointed* your gift, other people will be impacted and directed toward God.

4. Seek counsel from mature Christians.

Mature Christians are not people who will tell you what you want to hear about a particular situation in your life; rather, they are people who know what the Word of God says about a particular situation and can discern what the Spirit of God is saying. Contrary to what many Christians may think, maturity is not determined by the number of years a person has been saved. It is determined by whether a person consistently makes decisions based on the Word of God.

Don't be afraid to submit your gift, calling, and destiny to mature people who are strong in the Word. Proverbs 20:18 (AMP) says, "Purposes and plans are established by counsel; and [only] with good advice make or carry on war." For example, a Believer may want to press ahead with his or her plans to marry a particular individual, without any counseling from older, mature Christians who can see things from a clearer perspective. When you refuse to seek counsel from godly people, you are setting yourself up for problems down the road. Don't hesitate to surround yourself with godly advice as you begin to fulfill what God has called you to do.

5. Listen to the witness of the Holy Spirit in your spirit.

A "witness" is that inner knowing, or "compass," in the depth of your spirit. When you have the witness in the person of the Holy Spirit, He will tell you that you are in the right place, that you are where you are supposed to be. He will also let you know when you're in the wrong place. Listen to the witness of the Holy Spirit before proceeding with any endeavor. The Spirit of God is your leader and guide through life. He knows where your destiny is, and if you will begin to listen to Him, He will save you money, time, energy, and trouble. He knows how to maximize the gifts God has placed in your life and connect you to the people and situations that can get you where you need to be.

The challenge that everyone faces in hearing from the Holy Spirit is being able to distinguish between God's voice and the voice of your flesh. Often people battle within themselves in this area. Know this: where you want to be is not always where you *need* to be. Once you get to the place where you are supposed to be and you *know* you are in the right place, God will put the desire to be there within you. However, if you continue pursuing something that is not His will, He will most likely take the desire for it away from you so that you will not want to be there any longer!

I know firsthand what it is like to be called to do something you don't want to do. When people would tell me I was going to preach the Gospel one day, I fought it with every fiber of my being. My plan was to play professional football, but God had a different course charted for my life. Proverbs 20:24 says that ultimately, the Lord is the one who directs your steps. He knows how to get you where you need to be.

6. Determine what you can (or can't) give yourself to—100 percent.

What is it that you can give yourself to—100 percent—in order to accomplish it, and what *can't* you give yourself to—100 percent—for the rest of your life? Determining this will eliminate things you may be trying to lend your energy to that aren't the will of God. Sometimes it takes experiencing what you *don't* want in order to determine what you *do* want.

I'm a preacher. It is my calling. I love to run my mouth, talk to people, and preach to them! To me, preaching is more than an occupation; it is my life. What in your life holds that position? There is something that you absolutely love to do, and can do without ever getting tired of it. Figure out what it is, and ask God how to develop in it.

There is something that you absolutely love to do, and can do without ever getting tired of it. Figure out what it is, and ask God how to develop in it.

---

7. Know what produces good fruit in your life.

What produces good fruit in your life? The things that God has called you to do will always produce favorable results. If you are pursuing something and it isn't producing anything in your life besides a bunch of wasted time and energy, that is a clear indication that you are in the wrong lane and need to be rerouted.

8. *Follow the peace of God inside you.*

God has an "umpire" of peace that He has placed in your spirit to guide you—the Holy Spirit. The Holy Spirit will call something either "safe" or "out." You will know what to do by the peace, or lack of peace, you feel in your spirit about a particular thing. You don't always have to know why you feel something is either "safe" or "out." Don't worry about trying to figure everything out; just follow that peace. If you feel an agitation or discomfort about something, don't ignore it—*stop!* Don't go any further in something when you don't have the peace of God about it. Colossians 3:15 says, "And let the peace of God rule in your hearts." As you begin to follow the peace in your spirit, God will show you exactly where you need to be.

There is a destiny that God has already planned for you, and if you don't neglect the seemingly small areas—the areas of teaching and training that God wants to take you through—you will find it. God is perfecting those things that concern you, and when you get in line with His will for your life and yield to the things He has put in you, your path will become more clear every day, until before you know it, you will be walking in the perfect will of God for your life.

Of course, the prerequisite to all these steps is to make a decision to give your life to Jesus Christ. He is the door to your destiny. You can't get any farther in life before you accept Him into your heart. Once you do, you can begin to walk out God's awesome plan for prosperity and live an adventurous life of faith.

Review Nuggets

Your success in life is directly connected to your purpose and destiny. God has predetermined something specific for you to accomplish. Rest assured that you will achieve success by discovering and walking in your purpose. Remind yourself often that God has a plan for your life and He wants you to discover what it is.

Review the eight steps to God's will in this chapter as often as necessary to stay on course. Remember, God will guide you along the way if you seek Him first, committing to His will above your own desires. These actions will help you arrive at your God-given destination!

Foundation Scripture

Before I formed thee in the belly I knew thee; and before thou camest forth out of the womb I sanctified thee, and I ordained thee a prophet unto the nations.

Jeremiah 1:5

Practical Application

Write down five things that excite you in life. Out of those five, pick one or two that you would love to do even if you weren't paid to do them. Write down how you can use those passions to help others, and execute a plan to begin using your gifts.

10 Questions for Uncovering Your Destiny

What is your purpose in life? Have you strongly considered why you're here, now, at this particular time? There is a *specific* reason why you were born, a specific thing only you can accomplish while you're here. It's your responsibility to discover what that reason is. You can position yourself to lock into your destiny by obeying Psalm 37:4, which says, "Delight thyself also in the LORD: and he shall give thee the desires of thine heart." That means that when you delight yourself in Him, seek Him, and make Him your first priority, He will not only put certain desires in your heart, but He will *fulfill* those desires.

Some people don't want to follow God's plan for their lives. They fear it will require something they don't want to do. What you must understand is that when *God* promises you the desires of your heart, it's because He put them there! This is why He can make such a blanket statement. In the process of walking to your destiny, His desires for your life become your desires. You will find that you now desire to do what He has prepared for your life. Not only will He fulfill it, but He will make it something you thoroughly enjoy!

There are ten questions you must ask yourself in order to uncover your destiny. These questions will get you on the path to your purpose and help you find out what God has called you to do. Have a pen and paper handy and write down whatever comes to you as you go through this list.

THE TEN QUESTIONS

1. What is the deepest desire of your heart?

Psalm 37:4 says that as you delight in knowing and serving God, the first thing He will do is place His desires within you. In putting certain desires in you, He will also take other desires out of you. You will find that the more you pursue God with your mind, body, and soul, the more the things that you thought you wanted will lose their appeal.

God will place certain desires in your heart, and fulfill them, too! Your confidence lies in the fact that if *God* puts a desire in your heart, in due season it will come to pass.

You may ask, "How do I know if a desire is from God?" One way is if it's something you can't seem to get away from, regardless of how hard you try. Often, if your spirit continues in the direction of that desire despite what things look like on the outside, it is a strong indication that the desire is from God. Some people spend years trying to run from the desires God has placed in them, in pursuit of what they think they want to do, but they always end up coming back to the true desire of their heart.

Now, some people think doing whatever you desire is selfish and it's more "spiritual" to do what you don't want to do. Think about that for a moment. Why would it be more spiritual for you to do what you don't want to do? Remember, when God puts something in your heart, He gives you the desire to do it as well. You can't ignore the things God has placed in your heart.

2. What stirs your passions?

Passion is that zeal, excitement, or intensity you feel about the things that are important to you. Jesus had zeal for the house of the Lord, and it was evidenced when He drove the moneychangers out of the temple. John 2:13–15 describes the action He took:

And the Jews' passover was at hand, and Jesus went up to Jerusalem. And found in the temple those that sold oxen and sheep and doves, and the changers of money sitting: And when he had made a scourge of small cords, he drove them all out of the temple, and the sheep, and the oxen; and poured out the changers' money, and overthrew the tables.

Jesus was pretty stirred up! So stirred up and moved by His intense passion for the house of God and the people of God that He took action. His passion moved Him to do something. When Jesus' disciples saw Him doing this, they were reminded of the Scripture (Psalm 69:9) that says, "For the zeal of thine house hath eaten me up; and the reproaches of them that reproached thee are fallen upon me." That's how it should be with the godly desires of your heart. Whether it is a problem you want to solve or something you see in society you just want to change, your desire should move you to take action.

When you discover your passion, you are on your way to discovering your destiny. God gave you that passion because He wants you to help solve the problem.

3. What gifts, anointing, and talents flow naturally through you?

Your course of destiny will feel right because it will flow naturally. Everyone has some skill that comes easily to them. What is it you do effortlessly and naturally? Maybe it's a skill or a talent you've had for a long time. What is easy for you but complex for someone else? Your calling is unique to you, and God wants to cultivate your gifts and talents so you can use them to benefit the Kingdom of God.

4. Do you seek the counsel of mature Christians?

What is a mature Christian? A mature Christian is not necessarily someone who has been saved for a long time. Rather, it is someone who makes every decision based on the Word of God. Surround yourself with mature Christians and leaders who make a habit of making decisions based on the Word of God. Proverbs 11:14 says there is safety in a multitude of counselors. Be willing to submit your vision and your gift to mature counsel. Proverbs 20:18 further says that every purpose is established by counsel. Proverbs 18:1 (AMP) says, "He who willfully separates and estranges himself [from God and man] seeks his own desire and pretext to break out against all wise and sound judgment." You set yourself up for failure by refusing the advice and counsel of mature Christians and leaders.

5. What is the witness of the Holy Spirit in your spirit?

There is yet another safeguard that God has placed in the life of every Christian to determine whether something is His will: His peace. Because you are a child of God, the Holy Spirit will bear witness with your born-again spirit that you are in your destiny.

When the Holy Spirit bears witness with your spirit that you are on the right path, you will have supernatural peace. On the other hand, when you are off track, you won't feel peace about proceeding. The Holy Spirit will hold you back, or prompt you to not move forward. Whatever you do, don't ignore the leading of the Holy Spirit. If something doesn't sit right with you, don't continue in it, expecting things to change. As much as it may hurt or disappoint you, follow your peace and move on.

6. What do other mature Christians see in you?

Sometimes Believers want to separate themselves from the wise people whom God has placed in their paths because they want to selfishly fulfill their own desires. Now I'm not saying that you should make your decisions based on what other people think, but it is wise to pay attention to what other mature Believers say about a situation. They have been through more than you have and have experience in areas you may be unaware of.

Don't surround yourself with people who just tell you what you want to hear. People make the biggest mistakes when they listen to what their friends have to say about their dreams and goals, rather than listening to what God has to say. Don't accept advice from individuals whose lives don't line up with the Word. They are not qualified to advise you on the best decisions to make for your life, if their own decisions are not in agreement with God.

7. What career or ministry do you feel the peace of God about pursuing?

We discussed the "umpire of peace" earlier, and He is so critical in determining your career path. Philippians 4:6, 7, Isaiah 26:3, and Colossians 3:15 discuss the peace of God. I can't emphasize enough how important it is to pay attention to the peace of God in your spirit before stepping out on anything! God already knows the final outcome of every situation in your life. The peace of God is a sure-fire indicator of whether you should move forward. Follow your peace and you will *never* go wrong.

8. What thoughts, visions, or dreams are impossible to put out of your mind?

There is something God has put in your heart that you simply can't get rid of, no matter how hard you try. Your path just seems to always come back to that particular thing, year after year. You may have thoughts, visions, and dreams about it every day. If you can identify that particular desire, you will be one step closer to your destiny.

Acts 2:17 describes the move of God that He promises will occur in the Last Days. It says, "And it shall come to pass in the last days, saith God, I will pour out of my Spirit upon all flesh: and your sons and your daughters shall prophesy, and your young men shall see visions, and your old men shall dream dreams." The Holy Spirit will give you dreams and visions, so don't think it strange if you have them because God may be trying to get your attention.

If your dream or vision lines up with God's Word and will help build the Kingdom of God and help people in some way, then it is a very real option for you to pursue.

9. To what can you give 100 percent of yourself, for your whole life?

This is a very important question, and it will help you weed out the job, career or business that is not a part of God's plan for you. There is a difference between something you are doing to pay the bills and the destiny God has laid out for you. A lot of people work at dead-end jobs they don't enjoy, stuck in a rut because they need the money. Listen, the good life goes far beyond this type of lifestyle. God will prosper you more than you could ever imagine, and He will allow you to do what you love at the same time. Take a look at what you are doing right now and consider whether it is something you could spend the rest of your life doing with zeal and gusto.

The good news is that when *God* places a dream or vision in your heart, you will never get tired of pursuing it. Your passion for it will never die down or fade out. That's how you know what you are truly called to do.

I know that I am called to the ministry, that I am called to preach and teach the Word of God with simplicity and understanding. It is a passion that will never go away. God even used the education that I obtained to help point me in the right direction. I have always loved helping people, and found myself regularly counseling others even as I went through college. My job at a psychiatric institute helped me hone my counseling skills. God used all of my educational and occupational experiences prior to becoming a pastor to help guide me toward my ultimate destiny in the ministry.

Because of my passion for what I do, I am able to keep going even when things get tough. I know that when it is time for me to go home to be with the Lord, I will have successfully finished my course. I'm doing what I love *and* fulfilling the call of God on my life. What is it that *you* can honestly give yourself to, 100 percent, for the rest of your life?

10. What do people want to gather around and help you accomplish?

In Acts 16:10, we see a description of the apostle Paul's vision from God. When everyone with him heard about it, they immediately got up and followed him as he stepped out on it. They were willing to support it wholeheartedly. "And after he had seen the vision, immediately we endeavoured to go into Macedonia, assuredly gathering that the Lord had called us for to preach the gospel unto them." These people didn't need Paul to try to convince them that he heard from God, because they knew beyond a shadow of a doubt that God was involved. This is how it should be with your vision.

When a vision or dream is God-inspired, other people will catch it and want to be part of it. They will want to support you. It won't be a situation where you have to convince others that you "heard from God" and try to get them to go along with it. Often, when you feel the need to do that, you are missing it. Whether it is a business idea, concept, invention, or ministry endeavor, Holy Spirit-inspired visions are convincing, and others will feel peace about supporting you. They will have a witness in their spirit and want to get involved.

God wants you to discover what you are supposed to be doing in life. By asking yourself these ten questions and taking the time to answer them honestly, you can find out what your purpose is and begin walking in it. Don't wait another day!

Review Nuggets

Uncovering your destiny is a step-by-step process. Together with the leading of the Holy Spirit, you will be able to discover and walk out your destiny.

Foundation Scripture

Delight thyself also in the Lord: and he shall give thee the desires of thine heart.

Psalm 37:4

Practical Application

The only way to discover God's plan for your life is to spend time with Him. Delighting yourself in God means you find satisfaction and pleasure in your fellowship with Him in prayer and the Word. It also means making the Word your final authority in life. Take time to examine your relationship with the Father. Do you have regular, intimate fellowship with Him?

Begin your day by spending ten to fifteen minutes in God's Word or in prayer. Write down in your journal anything God speaks to you. He will reveal His will for you during these special times of fellowship.

Conclusion

I pray that this book has provided clear understanding about how to locate your destiny and has given you the tools you need to fulfill all God has called you to do. Though religion may tell you that being broke, sick, or in lack is "godly" and pleases the Father, the truth is, God desires for you to prosper and live the good life. That's why Jesus came to Earth! He has made a way for you to be wealthy and prosperous in every area of your life.

The Word is your foundation for prosperity. Only by making the Bible your first priority and your final authority will you begin to walk in the overflow of God's blessings. I encourage you to renew your thinking by meditating on God's promises so you can experience the overflow of prosperity in your life.

Renew your thinking by meditating on God's promises so you can experience the overflow of prosperity in your life.

Once you change your mindset, you will change your life. It all begins with the words you receive into and speak out of your heart. Your thoughts, emotions, feelings, decisions, actions, habits, and character will follow. To ensure that you reach the right destination in life, make sure everything you do is in agreement with God's Word. This is your guaranteed recipe for success.

There is a preordained and specific path God has designed for your life. It is up to you to *discover*, and choose, the path you take. Discover what God has planned for you by spending time with Him in prayer and in His Word. Evaluate your deepest desires and passions. Use the ten questions in Chapter 30 as signposts to point you to your destination. Don't allow confusion to distract you from your purpose. Seek and remain focused on the Word of God to experience the good life and every blessing that comes with it!

Seek and remain focused on the Word of God to experience the good life and every blessing that comes with it!

About the Author

Dr. Creflo A. Dollar is the dynamic founder of World Changers Church International (WCCI), a global ministry organization anchored by its world-renowned church in College Park, Georgia, with nearly 30,000 members. Dr. Dollar's life goal is to bring the Good News of Jesus Christ to people of every color and culture, literally changing the world one person at a time. The award-winning *Changing Your World* television broadcast now reaches nearly one billion homes on a vast network of stations in practically every country in the world.

Dr. Dollar founded the Creflo Dollar Ministerial Association (CDMA) to assist ministers, pastors, evangelists, ministry leaders, and churches large and small in the fulfillment of their God-given visions. Members have access to a long list of benefits, support services, and ministry resources designed to optimize their effectiveness on the "how-to's" of ministry, providing opportunities to network with like-minded men and women of God.

Dr. Dollar is a much sought-after conference speaker and a best-selling author. He has written books on a variety of topics, including debt cancellation, healing, total-life prosperity, prayer, marriage, child-rearing, the Christian family, and victorious living. Many of his past works, including *The Anointing to Live, Understanding God's Purpose for the Anointing, No More Debt* and *Uprooting the Spirit of Fear,* have been added to the curricula of Christian colleges across the United States. In addition, Dr. Dollar is the publisher of *CHANGE* magazine, a quarterly publication with nearly 100,000 subscribers, and *The Max,* a bimonthly resource newsletter for ministers and ministry leaders.

In addition to his regular appearance on the *Changing Your World* broadcast, Dr. Dollar maintains an extensive schedule of partner meetings, conventions, and speaking engagements in locations that span the globe. "When I see all of the people in this world who are hurting, it just motivates me to do more," he says. "The job is not done until every single person on the planet has been exposed to this Gospel."

Other Books by Dr. Creflo A. Dollar